Fresh Ideas for
ADMINISTRATION & FINANCE

FOR

ADMINISTRATION & FINANCE

WORD BOOKS
PUBLISHER
WACO, TEXAS

A DIVISION OF
WORD, INCORPORATED

Christianity Today, Inc.
Carol Stream, Illinois

Edited by Dean Merrill and Marshall Shelley
Designed by Tim Botts

© 1982, 1983, 1984 Christianity Today, Inc.
Published by Christianity Today, Inc.
465 Gundersen Drive, Carol Stream, IL 60188
Printed in the United States of America
ISBN 0-917463-01-3

C O N T E N T S

INTRODUCTION

Welcome to a smorgasbord of fresh ideas for the local church.

This book — and the other three in the series — have been created to give pastors and lay leaders solutions. Few problems in church life are unique; most challenges have cropped up somewhere else — and been conquered. It's only logical, then, to share creative answers with one another. If a solution has already been tried and proven in Gainesville or Rochester, why reinvent it in Ponca City?

Contrary to popular opinion, there *is* innovation and creativity in the churches across the United States and Canada. This book showcases that creativity.

As you read the many short vignettes and the longer features, you'll find some that contain several ideas you can use, others only one. Sometimes a single sentence will trigger a brainstorm with which you can attack a particular problem you're facing. The point is not to swallow these ideas whole but rather to tailor them to your situation, adapting, modifying, and even improving as you go.

Most of the reports here were first published during 1982-83 in a magazine called *Leadership 100*. Similar material from *Leadership* Journal has been added to this collection. While not all ideas may be still in place as described here, and no doubt there have been personnel changes in some churches, we believe the value of the ideas stands intact.

As you read, enjoy the good news that churches are doing some things *right* — and help yourself to the creativity, which has its ultimate source not in any human mind but in God alone.

DEAN MERRILL
Senior Editor, *Leadership*

THE OFFICE
AND STAFF

What Volunteer Secretaries Need Most

What's the key to maximizing volunteer office help? Can unpaid secertaries be relied upon to show up faithfully and not make costly mistakes? Two churches — one very large, the other small — say yes.

Chapel Rock Christian Church in Indianapolis draws over 1,600 on Sunday morning, has a ministerial staff of five, two morning services, eight choirs, 15 elders, 140 lay shepherds — and *one* paid secretary. The rest of the desk work is carried by 11 volunteers.

"There are a lot of fine women in churches who were exceptional secretaries in the business world," says senior minister Dennis Fulton. "Their childbearing years came along, and now they are not going back to work and don't want to. But they count it a joy to come work for the church half a day each week."

Thus, each Chapel Rock volunteer serves as the office receptionist/switchboard operator and also carries a definite assigned work load as follows:

Monday a.m.: Collects all roll call cards and sorts into members and nonmembers. Processes all information from cards to ministers or the full-time secretary. Sends information report to national church magazine.

Monday p.m.: Alphabetizes visitor cards. Posts regular visitors' attendance. Checks for first-timers. Consults with secretary to see who should receive a visitor letter.

Tuesday a.m.: Records the previous week's home calls and prepares calling cards from the first-timer list.

Tuesday p.m.: Alphabetizes member roll call cards.

Posts attendance in shepherding books.

Wednesday a.m.: Prepares new-member packets for those who joined the church the previous Sunday. Makes address changes for shepherding and notifies shepherds. Sends weekly prayer letter.

Wednesday p.m.: Files all roll call cards, calling cards, etc.

Thursday a.m.: Makes address plates for new members and those who've moved. Makes phone calls for new-member pictures.

Thursday p.m.: Assembles booklets. Handles Cradle Roll mail.

Friday a.m.: Does last-minute typing, library work.

Friday p.m.: Stuffs bulletins for Sunday. (Church has a paid printer.)

Saturday a.m.: Keeps all shepherding records.

This system has been running smoothly for more than a decade. "It takes a definite commitment," says one woman who has worked from the beginning, "but we've settled into the routine of it now end enjoy making a contribution to the church."

Says Dennis Fulton, "*Volunteer* is really a misnomer, because we don't just issue a general plea for help. We hand-pick the people and try them out first on special projects, like bulk mailings or collating a book. We prove whether they are capable and adaptable before asking them to donate their time.

"So what we have are not volunteer secretaries — they're *selected* secretaries. They have really freed our staff — and our budget — for growth in ministry."

When the paid secretary at Trinity Temple Bible Church in Fort Smith, Arkansas, resigned, this church of 100 decided to put the salary dollars into a youth leader instead. The office needs were turned over to a corps of volunteers like Chapel Rock's, but with one difference: 10 women work mornings only on a two-week rotation.

"Each lady brings a variety of different skills," says

Pastor Edward Eaton. "Some are better at typing and mimeographing. Some excel at making telephone arrangements. Some are best at filing. I assign them work based on their abilities, so each one can feel she's done the task well."

Suzie Schmidly, the lay coordinator who recruited the workers, gives high marks to the pastor's planning. "That's been the secret — the way he matches up the work," she says. "Some of the women can't type at all, so they do filing instead. The two or three whiz typists handle the correspondence."

Another crucial detail: before leaving each noon, the volunteer phones tomorrow's worker to remind her. Since the cycle is not an every-week rhythm, this phone call is important to ensure that everyone shows up as scheduled.

"Our workers range from 19-year-olds to grandmothers," says Schmidly. "And it's really worked out smoothly."

Senior Secretaries

While the elderly have helped in many kinds of volunteer service, churches have often hesitated to involve them as secretaries. Could they fit into the sometimes hectic life of an office? Would they be fast enough? Is there too much lifting, walking, and overall exertion for a retired person? What about operating complicated equipment?

One pastor who has had nothing but good experience using senior secretaries is Paul Hendricks, pastor until recently of Arbutus Baptist Church outside Baltimore. Two women in their late sixties took turns with a 9 A.M. to 1 P.M. shift, one working two days a week, the other three. "I found them to be just what we needed," says Hendricks, who now serves the Jessup

Baptist Church, also in Maryland. "They were especially good at arranging things by telephone, setting up meetings, and reminding people of assignments. They functioned fine, whether I was in the office or not."

Hendricks did not issue a general call to his older members' group (they called themselves the "Keen-Agers") for volunteers; instead, he approached the women he thought would be likely candidates. One had been a secretary with a trucking company during her earning years, the other an industrial nurse. Thus, careful recruitment helped ensure successful placement.

"Even though the church couldn't afford a paid secretary, I knew we had a wealth of unrecognized resource sitting in the pews," Hendricks adds. "Over the years, this job produced a sense of usefulness for these two women and brought them public honor for their help to the church and the pastor."

A Secretary for Sunday

"For want of a secretary, the contact was lost."

That's not quite the way Benjamin Franklin phrased his maxim, but most pastors would vouch for the truth: Sunday — the hub of the week — is the worst possible day to be without a secretary.

At the Eglise de Pentecôte in Drummondville, Quebec, the four pastors have been smiling every since Guylaine Blanchard began working Sunday morning and taking Monday morning off. An active member of the church, she's there for morning worship anyway, and she stays afterward as long as needed (usually no more than an hour).

"What better time than Sundays," says Pastor Claude Favreau, to . . .

• distribute information packets, memos, and correspondence to members of the congregation;

- prepare birth certificates;
- collect data from members and visitors — addresses, phone numbers, names of children, etc.;
- answer miscellaneous questions.

"This makes the secretary visible to the congregation and lets them deal directly with her at their point of greatest convenience. They get to chat with her and appreciate what she does. Meanwhile, it frees us pastors from details so we can concentrate on ministry."

As for Guylaine Blanchard's opinion: "I'm not here because I have to — I want to. It's a very efficient time to work. I can accomplish more things faster on Sunday after church than at any other hour, because people are available.

"And then, there's always the joy of sleeping in on Monday morning!"

Sunday Morning Mail

One of the nagging irritations of any pastor is getting home after a busy Sunday and suddenly remembering, "Oh, I forgot to tell Mrs. Johnson about . . ."

When David Goodman was pastor at Grace Brethren Church in Bowling Green, Ohio, and later at Grace Brethren in Anaheim, California, he found that even though the churches had only 100 on Sunday mornings, getting messages to specific individuals was a problem.

"Each week dozens of ideas, corrections, and encouragements that needed to be made would crowd into my mind and promptly be lost in the shuffle of sermon preparation and delivery," he says.

"The best solution was the simplest one. I asked someone — in each case an older woman who knew everyone in the congregation — to be a mail carrier. The ladies were delighted to serve this way."

During the week, Goodman would write notes to board members, sort mail that came for the nursery co-ordinator or missions committee, and forward information about teaching workshops to Sunday school workers — knowing it all would be delivered on Sunday. This left his mind free to concentrate on ministry.

"I didn't ask the church secretary to parcel out the messages, because enough people harass her on Sunday as it is," he says.

Do people resent being contacted like this rather than in person?

"Rather than being seen as impersonal," Goodman says, "most people appreciate a personal note from the pastor. They see it as an organized way of spreading information and checking on needs."

Remembering Good Decisions

What good does it do for the membership to set a policy on something if no one remembers it two years later when the issue comes up?

Ilene H. Herst, administrator of the K.A.M. Isaiah Israel Congregation on Chicago's South Side, has thought about that problem. "If the decision is buried in a set of minutes somewhere," she says, "I can't get to it unless someone remembers (a) that the subject did come up once, and (b) the approximate date of discussion. Otherwise, the decision is lost."

Her solution: "Before filing each set of minutes in the record book, I photocopy them and cut them up, putting each item on a separate file card. At the top of the card, I put the subject and the date of the congregational meeting. Then I file the cards by subject.

"This file box stays right next to my desk for easy access. I never have to look far to find all the motions pertaining to any specific area."

An Active Sitting Ministry

With more and more women working, Community Baptist Church in Alta Loma, California, found that more and more people were phoning in to ask for reputable baby sitters and day care help.

"August and September are especially busy, and December is another peak time," say Janet Logan, communications secretary. "In the fall, when school starts, people lose their sitters, and many times people have just moved in during the summer and don't know where to turn for child care. In December, vacations disrupt normal sitting schedules, so people turn to the church for referrals."

So in each Rolodex around the church offices, there's a list of baby sitters. One section is for high school students who want to sit evenings. Another section lists women who do child care for working mothers. And still another section is for those who will care for children in extended situations such as business trips.

"Many of our calls are from unchurched people," says Logan, "especially new residents. By providing faithful sitters, we have an outreach. Often the sitters are able to take a personal interest in the family, befriend them, and invite them to church."

THE RESEARCH ASSISTANT

by Donald L. Bubna, pastor, Salem Alliance Church, Salem, Oregon

Most pastors would be intrigued by the prospect of an assistant to develop their file systems and do research on sermon materials.

If you react, "Sounds like a great idea, but our church doesn't have the money," don't stop reading yet. It's not really a money matter.

I've had such an assistant for years. She has enriched my life and found new purpose and ministry for herself. And like other church volunteers, she has never received a salary.

Verna Sturdivant and her husband, Clair, moved to our city over a decade ago to retire. A former schoolteacher, Verna was a lover of books and wanted to remain intellectually active. Her responses to my messages revealed a thinking and appreciative hearer as well as a "doer of the Word."

One day she told me about some E. Stanley Jones readings that paralleled certain points of my most recent sermon. I asked to see them and realized how much they would have enhanced that message.

"Verna," I said, "would you be willing to help me by looking for this type of material in advance?"

She accepted eagerly, and we began.

Frankly, that put me under a bit of pressure. If Verna were to help me effectively, I needed to know fairly well ahead of time what I would be preaching on. I saw I needed to grow. This new accountability would be good for me.

Soon, I was discussing with Verna very early each week ideas for the next Sunday's message, and she was supplying beautiful materials from her own library — illustrations of devotional excerpts that ideally augmented my sermons.

It became obvious that I should work even further in advance. This took a while, but now it is my common practice to prepare outlines a month in advance. These outlines often undergo radical changes during the month, but they serve as a starting point and use Verna's gifts of research. In addition, I've found that communicating with her in person or in writing helps solidify my ideas earlier.

Next, Verna investigated the poorly organized material in my church study. The Bubna system of book filing meant the most-used books were closest to me. This worked fine when my library numbered only a few hundred. Verna, however, began to discover treasures I had somehow forgotten because they had been relegated to the back corner of the shelf.

She decided my books should be catalogued according the the Dewey Decimal system. Her determination was undimmed by previous inexperience. We ordered several how-to books, and our local librarian also seemed delighted to help out.

After conquering the book file, Verna began the task of integrating my file material of magazine articles, cutouts, and old notes into a usable sytem. She worked several years perfecting this, ultimately cataloguing it using Baker's Textual and Topical Filing System.

Several years ago, I prepared to study for a series on the Minor Prophets but lacked materials in my study. In a few days, Verna presented a briefcase of books she had borrowed from a nearby Christian college. It didn't take me long to scan them and decide which ones to use, perhaps even to purchase.

Her quest for illustrations, background material on contemporary issues, and half-forgotten quotes takes her to such sources as the Reader's Guide to Periodical Literature at the public library. A faithful reader of E. Stanley Jones and *Daily Bread* devotionals, Verna often finds illustrations that are helpful to me either at the time or some later point.

When her husband passed away, she began to give even more time to this work. Now in her late seventies, Verna no longer drives her car but arrives via city bus or with someone she has convinced to drive her!

Sometimes I have wondered if I were taking advantage of this dear sister. But she assures me she loves it all. Over the years, we have become very good friends, and at times I have been her counselor. On one such occasion, she gave me permission to talk with her doctor. He commented on her growing zest for life and attributed her physical well-being to her church work.

"Verna has told me something of what she is doing for you," he said. "I don't understand it all, but whatever it is, don't let it stop! It's given her added years of purposeful service."

Verna is now trying to recruit and train younger women to supplement her efforts.

Each congregation has gifted people who would love to help the pastor as a research assistant. To find those who might be interested and well-qualified: Listen for clues. Ask provocative questions and give short-term assignments. Offer lots of encouragement and appreciation.

Give your ministry a boost, and at the same time allow someone else the meaningful service of helping you declare the Word of God.

Perfect Memory—Instantly

The minutes immediately after the worship service are a jumble of names, messages, and greetings.

"Pastor, my son is in the hospital for tests. Could you see him sometime this week?"

"These are our new neighbors, the Crumleys. They're interested in finding a church home."

"Could you ask the church to pray for my husband? He's getting laid off next week."

George Granberry, associate pastor at Calvary Church in Longmont, Colorado, was finding it hard to remember everything people would tell him after Sunday services.

"Names of visitors, people in the hospital, even prayer requests were being given me in that brief encounter of shaking hands at the door," he says.

His solution: a microcassette recorder. It's small enough to slip into a shirt pocket, and the 60 minutes-per-side cassette is more than enough for the post-service mingling.

"All the comments come through surprisingly clear. Then, on Monday before staff meeting, I listen to the tape, jot down the information and requests, and report anything that needs to be followed up. I'm able to remember faces of visitors as I hear their voices," says Granberry.

"The recorder, which costs around $60, allows me to relax while talking to people, not struggle to memorize every detail. It also saves me the embarrassment of having to say, 'I forgot.' "

Pocket Pagers: a Good Idea?

Should a pastor carry a beeper device when he's out of the office? Or is his life dominated by the telephone enough as it is?

Calvin Marcum, former pastor of First Presbyterian Church in Aurora, Illinois, is a firm believer in the value of a paging service — *if* combined with a discerning secretary who knows when to use it. "I find it tremendously liberating," says Marcum. "I'm never out of touch; I never have to worry that I'm missing something important."

Like most pastors, he gets the full range of incoming calls, from the deadly serious to the trivial. Some people even ask to talk to the senior pastor in order to find out what time the services are. My secretary, naturally, tries to divert these kinds of calls, but she always has the option of saying, 'I'm sorry, he's out of the office this afternoon; would you like for me to page him?' People usually don't say yes unless it's really important."

Members and other callers are thus impressed by the fact that, although the pastor is busy at his work, he is still as close as the nearest pay telephone if they truly need him.

At Calvary Memorial Church in nearby Oak Park, an added use for the pager has been discovered: it substitutes for an intercom system within the church building. "One of our secretaries came up with the bright idea of letting the custodian wear it while I'm in the office," says Pastor Donald Gerig. "That way, whenever there's a message or a need, they don't have to dash around the building trying to locate him. One phone call activates the pager, and he promptly shows up."

Gerig also uses the device to screen calls when he's alone in his office during the evening. "I finally convinced myself to ignore the telephone, since emergency calls would probably go to the parsonage anyway. Then my wife can activate the pager if I'm truly needed right away; otherwise, I just go on working."

Paging service is available in most cities over 200,000 and covers up to a 60-mile radius. The monthly fee: $20-30.

Making Sure Your Books Come Back

Most pastors would be more than glad to loan their books — *if* they could be sure of getting them back.

J. L. Rivera, pastor of Christian Fellowship Church in Chicago, loans out his books constantly and says, "I haven't lost a book in six years." How does he do it? He simply disciplines himself to keep a four-by-seven index card in his desk on which he jots the title of every outgoing book, who's borrowing it, and the date.

"That way I always know where my books are. I don't try to rely on my memory. I want to make good Christian books available to my people, and this little system frees me to do that.

"If I need a certain book for a sermon I'm preparing, I know immediately who to call. I can also tell who's had a book for a month or so and needs a reminder to return it."

Found but Forgotten

"I know I visited the Baltzers a few months ago, but how did I get there? Where in the world is Alcott Court?

"Let's see, the Vincents are out on Highway 63, but what's that turnoff?"

For pastors in tangled urban or suburban areas, or new pastors with a widely scattered congregation of farmers, remembering the way to infrequently visited places can be a challenge.

Donnie Whitney, pastor of Glenfield Baptist Church in the Chicago suburb of Glen Ellyn, has found a way to save the time and possible embarrassment of repeatedly calling for directions.

"Whenever I get directions," says Whitney, "I write them down on an index card. Then, after the visit, I put them in my 'directions' file.

"This would also be beneficial for multiple-staff churches where each staffer only occasionally visits certain hospitals, supply stores, or homes of members," he says.

Over the River and Through the Woods

If you're a new pastor in a rural area, who knows how to find every farmhouse, cabin, and bungalow in your parish?

The U.S. Geological Survey does.

When John Baker came from southern Ohio to Palo Congregational Church in the Iron Range of northern Minnesota, he found himself staring at a membership list with addresses no more helpful than "Route 1, Aurora," and "Route 1, Makinen."

"That's when I went looking for the topographical quadrangle maps published by the government," he says. "They're inexpensive, and they're large-scale; they show all roads, streams, lakes, and swamps as well as houses, outbuildings, churches, and cemeteries. I've been able to write in family names, plot in new homes, and identify the best routes for visitation trips. The maps are invaluable to me."

If a quadrangle includes a town, all streets are shown, although not by name. Every area has a local source of these maps, says Baker, which can be found by writing: Map Information Office, Geological Survey, Washington, DC 20242.

BOARDS AND COMMITTEES

HOW MANY COMMITTEES?

*For this Louisville church, there had to be a simpler way —
and there was.*

Ten years ago, administration at Bethlehem Baptist
Church in Louisville, Kentucky, was almost paralyzed. A total
of 61 different committees were trying to keep from
bumping into one another.

Today, the 2,200-member congregation has put its
affairs in the hands of three streamlined commissions. Yet no
one can accuse the church of being run by a junta. Bethlehem has successfully reorganized itself to overcome bureaucracy without slipping into the opposite ditch of
dictatorship.

"Shortly before I came in 1973," says Pastor Ralph
Hodge, "they realized something had to be done: the old system had become so inept that it demanded more than it was
providing. Committees spent most of their time struggling to
justify their existence.

"The previous pastor designed the alternative but left before it was functional. My job was to make it work. Now,
we're firm believers in its efficiency."

The system revolves around three administrative groups,
with each member specializing in an assigned area.

The *Worship Commission* deals with personal and corporate worship. Its members are:

Chairman	Lord's Supper chairman
Baptism chairman	New membership chairman
Drama chairman	Parking chairman
Finance chairman	Ushers chairman

The *Ministry Commission* concentrates on nonworship areas: It has a:

Chairman
Activities chairman (*the church has a multipurpose gym*)
Education chairman
Nursery chairman
Pastoral ministry chairman
Personnel chairman
Public relations chairman
Radio-television chairman

The *Mission Commission* guides the church's outreach. It includes a:

Chairman
Community Bible study and missions chairman
Home and foreign missions chairman
Institutional chaplaincies chairman
Mission organizations (children, teen, adult) chairman
Special ministries chairman (Alcoholics Anonymous, day care, crisis counseling center, food/clothing needs, etc.)

The three main chairmen are appointed by Pastor Hodge and the deacon chairman. Then the three nominate the rest of their respective commissions.

Once the commissions go to work, they continually pass around the moderator's hat depending on the subject at hand. If, for example, the Ministry Commission is plotting a series of newspaper ads, the public relations chairman runs the meeting. If the next agenda item is salary review, the personnel chairman takes over.

What keeps the commissions from turning into power cliques?

"The check on their power," says Hodge, "is that I have covenanted with the church that absolutely *everything* will be reported. We have a business meeting every month, after a Wednesday evening service. Members get a 15-20 page report that tells them what we've been up to, and anything they don't approve of can be stopped in short order. Nothing is slipped by in the shadows; everything is out in the open.

"As a result, there is a tremendous level of trust in the church. Commission recommendations are usually passed with ease; people are pleased with how thorough the reports are. Our business meetings generally take all of 10 minutes."

Bethlehem also has deacons, but their work is entirely pastoral. Each gives care to about 30 families, leaving the administrative detail to the three commissions.

The commission structure is purposely not a part of the church by-laws. "We want to be able to make changes as needed in order to meet current needs," Hodge explains.

"And we also bring in extra people to serve temporarily. Some 60 persons help form the annual budget, for example. We recently faced the need to dismiss a staff member. I had the power constitutionally to do it myself, but I chose to confer with the personnel chairman, who created an ad hoc committee for that situation, to make sure we were doing the necessary thing.

"We're in a building project at the moment, and the property chairman has asked 16 members to help him oversee that."

Hodge meets with his three main chairmen monthly to receive each commission's reports and prepare for the upcoming business meeting. The net result is that two dozen or so capable people are managing Bethlehem Baptist smoothly and effectively, subject always to the review of the large and growing membership.

Not every church would organize its commissions or individual chairmanships as this church has done, of course. But the combination of a lean governance structure with frequent reporting is worth the study of any congregation. "Our slogan has been 'Organize for Excellence,' " says Hodge. "I don't know of another church that does it quite this way, but I believe God has helped us find a structure that has let his work go forward."

One-Night Administration

Committee meetings are sometimes dreary affairs — a few dedicated souls trudging to one room of an otherwise dark and cavernous church building.

Several churches have brightened the atmosphere and also increased the efficiency by bunching all the monthly committee/board meetings onto one night. Here's how it works:

At First Union Presbyterian Church in Luling, Louisiana, committee night begins at 7 P.M. with coffee and conversation. Pastor Eddie L. Wells points out, "When a committee gathers by itself at the church, the members sometimes feel they're carrying the whole church on their shoulders. But when our leaders see 50 other decision makers, they know they're sharing the load."

After about 15 minutes, the eight committees convene, and Wells drops in on each meeting. "I seldom stay more than five minutes," he says with a smile. "I simply make my presence known, listen to what's going on, and lend a word of comment if asked. You can do this in five minutes — unless you want to sit around and try to convince everyone to do things *your* way."

Since the committees meet at the same time and place, they can communicate easily. Last year, for instance, the senior high sponsors met with the Christian education committee to see about setting up a youth worship serivce. Wells suggested they clear the matter with the worship committee. The two groups met. The members asked questions, gave suggestions, and all the details were worked out before the evening was over.

Wells has a lot more free time now. "But at first I felt a big void because I didn't know everything that was going on," he says. "I'd ask myself, 'I wonder what they're doing. Are they handling things right?' "

To remedy this, he has each committee complete its monthly report the same week of the Monday meeting.

Copies are circulated among the church elders, and Wells studies the reports himself. If he has questions or comments, he contacts the committee chairpersons immediately.

First Baptist Church, Ballston Spa, New York, approaches one-night administration this way:

• The church's four boards — deacon, trustee, Christian education, ministry — meet, but the many committees do not.

• The 15 minutes preceding the board meetings are used for a corporate devotional, not an informal fellowship.

"The first 15 minutes set the mood for the evening," says Stephen Holland, associate pastor. Pastor Nelson Elliott usually shares comments that stress the importance of serving the church through the various board functions.

After the 36 board members go to their separate places, the pastors choose to attend one meeting. They stay for the duration.

Like Wells, Holland stresses communication as the most practical benefit.

One night, for instance, the board of Christian education discussed the purchase of New International Version Bibles for the Sunday school. Students were bringing three different versions, making lessons unnecessarily difficult. The deacons had to be consulted before the purchase was made, but since they were on the premises, the matter was taken care of that evening.

Another time, a Sunday school teacher was doing a very poor job. The problem had more to do with deep personal problems than incompetence. The seriousness of the situation warranted the deacon board's intervention, since the Christian education board's responsibility extended only as far as teaching proficiency was concerned. Thus, the referral was made that night, and steps to correct the situation ensued immediately.

A similar plan functions at Trinity Church in El Monte, California, where all committees and the women's guild board meet one week prior to the meeting of the consistory, which oversees them.

"At the end of the evening we coordinate calendars for the last half hour," says Pastor Wayne Hoglin. "Any conflicts are ironed out right away, so that written reports can be completed that very night. The consistory members receive them the following Sunday, before their own meeting."

The advantages of holding all monthly committee meetings on one night:

- *Leaders have a special monthly time for fellowship.*
- *Since the pastor can't be at every meeting, the chairpersons are more inclined to take responsibility.*
- *Committees can more easily communicate and act on business that overlaps.*
- *The pastor is freed to spend more time with his family in the evenings.*

No Marathons

Everyone's in favor of shorter board meetings; the only question is how to get all the business done.

At the Church of the Nazarene in Newberg, Oregon, they simply set the adjournment time in advance — and make the work fit.

Bill O'Connor made this novel suggestion at the very first board meeting when he came to pastor the church in 1977. The group decided to start at 7:30 each month and quit at 9:30, period.

Does this result in railroading, or in work begin neglected? Not really, says O'Connor. He lists the following benefits:

- "We don't waste time endlessly discussing simple issues and decisions."

- "We keep an eye on the clock and make sure our important business is taken care of *early* in the meeting. We don't leave the heavy items till last."
- "Items that don't achieve a consensus of opinion are usually tabled until the next meeting."
- "Board members are more willing to apply themselves when they know they'll not be at the church half the night."

In fact, this 16-person board has gotten to the point where the printed agenda consumes only half the available time. The first hour of the meeting is given to a devotional (led by a different member each month), sharing needs, a prayer time, and a leadership discipling study/discussion. They actually "get down to business" around 8:30.

The only way a meeting can be extended is by majority vote, and then for a specified period of time. This allows for exceptional circumstances, but the norm is to wrap up at 9:30 and head for home.

Shorter Board Meetings? It's Possible

The elders of Community Bible Chapel in Richardson, Texas, are burning a lot less midnight oil these days. And they're still finishing the agenda.

What's the secret? "Homework," says Ed Martin, the church's program coordinator. For every topic that needs attention, "I press the presenting person to do some homework. That is, I ask him to do whatever research is necessary in order to put together a written report."

Most reports have two sections: (1) an analysis of the need, problem, or fact, and (2) a recommendation for action. Each report is mailed to the elders several days *before* the meeting, to be read and digested. If questions arise, an elder often phones the report writer to get clarification.

Once the group assembles, it doesn't have to spend time *informing* and *describing* — it can get right to *deciding*.

For example, a multi-page report on an upcoming vacation Bible school outlined many specifics: staffing, dates and times, materials needed, budget. The actual board meeting time required for a decision was "about 45 seconds," Martin says. If the group had tried to talk it all through, an hour could easily have been consumed.

"True, this method requires more time outside the elders' meetings. But since that work can be done within one's own schedule, the elders find it a very positive trade-off."

And the best reward of all, according to Martin, is that "with this kind of efficiency, there's even time to pray."

A Name for Every Task

Efficient meetings are one thing; good follow-through is quite another. In order to guarantee their decision making, the Richardson, Texas, elders make it crystal-clear in the minutes who's to do what.

For example:

DVBS Proposal, by John D. A written report mailed to the elders April 7. New cost estimate submitted by Paul C. is $750. The elders quickly agreed to have John put his plan into action.

ACTION: Ed M. will contact John D. this week to proceed with his DVBS plans, including revised cost estimate.

"I listen very carefully to the discussions to make sure the decisions reached are precise," says Ed Martin, who serves as recording secretary. "Unless I can pin down a specific name and exactly what that person is to do, I try not to let the issue rest.

"This written format — with the word **ACTION** in bold letters — makes the assignment jump out of the page.

"Also, by keeping the name of the person at the first of the sentence, it's easy to check off the responsiblities."
Adapted with permission from Pastoral Renewal

The Breakfast Board

Too often a board meeting matches the old proverb about paperwork: it expands to fill all available time.

Horror stories are legion about deacons' meetings stretching into the wee hours of the morning — and patience and friendships wearing out as the night wears on.

Franklin Congregational Christian Church in Virginia has never had that problem, at least not since they began holding the monthly deacons' meetings on Sunday morning — *before* Sunday school.

"We meet at 8 o'clock for breakfast, start talking business about 8:30, and everyone knows we have to be done by 9:30," says Pastor Richard Diekmann. "Our work proceeds smoothly, discussion focuses on the essentials, and there's no personal posturing or time wasting."

Each month, responsibility for breakfast rotates among the 12 deacons, with some preferring to serve it in their homes, other handling it in the church fellowship hall.

"On our board, the work of God in the church transcends factions and little games that create problems," says Diekmann. "We trust one another. And enjoying breakfast with one another before talking business adds to that atmosphere."

SIX PASTORS TELL HOW HARMONY CAME TO THEIR BOARDS

Are pastors and elders the natural prey of each other?
Can deacon meetings be friendly?
Must peace at the conference table await the Millennium?

In churches large and small, east and west, denominational and independent, pastors and lay leaders who have tired of the cold war are finding a better way. Part of the thaw is due to procedural change, while other aspects can only be attributed to a deep, internal work of the Holy Spirit.

Not all of the following ideas can be copied in every church; none of them is the "the only way." They are merely examples of what is working in a half-dozen situations.

Mornings Are Better

● *Dick Emery, Wesleyan Church of the Valley, Bonita, California:* "A key to our growth" (from 50 to 250 in six years) "has been the consistent steps of faith in which our board of administration has led the way. And I really believe that meeting on Saturday mornings, when everyone is fresh, instead of an evening after a long day of work, has been a factor.

"We are all just a lot more positive in the mornings. We gather at 7:00 for breakfast in the fellowship hall on the second Saturday of each month. We eat together, we talk, we spend about 15 minutes in prayer and sharing, and then we get to our business. By 9:00, we're finished. I am convinced it would take us longer in the evening, and the atmosphere would be entirely different."

First Things First

● *Lance C. Dallaire, United Churches of Christ in Fonda and Pomeroy, Iowa:* "We open every council meeting with 10 minutes or so of personal sharing. I ask one or two members in advance to come with a thought, idea, piece of poetry, Scripture, or personally written piece that means something special to him or her. Throughout a year's time, we work through the entire board.

"In this way, we come to know one another more closely. We understand each other better; we grow closer in Christ. And the business that follows doesn't become so formal."

● *Duane Coller, Open Bible Church, Boone, Iowa:* "When the board of elders meets, it is first of all a time of fellowship, prayer, and teaching. Before we discuss any business, we come together in spirit through praying for each other and the church body, sharing the Word together, and sharing the vision God has given us for our growth and maturity as a body."

A Commitment to Unanimous Decision Making

● *Duane Coller continues:* "With this as an essential backdrop, we have not made one decision in the last eighteen months that has not been unanimous. If we are unsure or split on a decision, we simply wait to act until we are agreed."

● *Jim Burgess, Fellowship Bible Church, Dalton, Georgia:* "When I came to this church, I followed an older man who had handled almost everything single-handedly. One of the first things I did was to preach a month of Sunday evening sermons on New Testament leadership, mainly from 1 and 2 Timothy and Titus. My ideas about multiple leadership were new to the people. When I said the Spirit could lead a pastor and deacon group as one, eyebrows went up.

"Right after the election of new deacons that fall, we

went on a weekend retreat to a cabin on a nearby mountain. We spent a lot of Friday evening just praying together, and on Saturday we talked about how we would function in the future. I could see some of the traditional tensions melting away.

"We committed ourselves to making only unanimous decisions, and we have done so since that time. In addition, one of the men suggested that we conclude every meeting with a prayer circle — arms around each other, praying for God's blessing upon us and the church. We've done that. As a result, we deeply love and care for each other."

● *Richard A. Laue, Calvary Bible Church, Burbank, California:* "After 17 years of pastoring in Indiana, I came here to a situation where the deacons and trustees had often battled each other. Each board could stymie the other, and did: as a result, the congregation was in frequent upheaval over the many split decisions.

"Fortunately, the lay leaders knew they couldn't go on like this and asked me, as part of the call, to guide them in reorganizing. I spent the first year just teaching the men of the church on discipleship. I painted the picture of what a true eldership would be. At the end of that year, both boards voted themselves out of existence.

"Eight elders were confirmed, and we decided all future decisions would be unanimous; the problems of the past had to be put behind us. The Lord has given us a harmonious and unified spirit. The monthly business meetings are a joy.

"We can't move as fast as we would like sometimes. It took us six months to come to consensus about buying two buses, for example. But the curious thing is that ministry, real ministry, goes on regardless. Our Sunday attendance has gone from 400 to 850 in the past five years. Our waiting and working toward agreement has not hindered the work of God; it has enhanced it."

● *Charles Colegrove, Fairview Apostolic Church, Grand Rapids, Michigan:* "We've learned not to push issues that aren't ready to be decided, just for the sake of finishing the agenda. In some cases I will adjourn the meeting long enough for each member to find a quiet place in the church and pray about the subject at hand. Then we will come together again.

"Not long ago we needed to select a teacher for the senior high Sunday school class. I recomended one person on the basis of his experience at teaching; I felt he could do a good job.

"But one of the deacons questioned whether he was active enough in the church to qualify for this position.

"Instead of battling out the pros and cons, we dismissed the board meeting to pray. I went to my office; the others went to various spots in the building. After about 20 minutes, we came together again, and we felt the Spirit had directed us all that the person should not be installed.

"Sometimes, if we still don't have oneness of opinion, we'll table the matter for another meeting. This gives time for emotions to cool, facts to be assembled, and more prayer to be offered."

A Separate Time to Pray Together

● *Jim Burgess:* "Another deacon proposed that we meet at some other time of each week just for prayer — no business. We chose Sunday afternoons at 5:30. The first half-hour we pray for each other; then we pray for the church."

● *Richard Laue:* "Our new eldership knew that we needed a way to develop in harmony. The Scriptures called us to be men of prayer and the Word, so we began meeting each Friday morning at 6:00 for an hour and a half of spiritual intercession, praise, and sharing. The congregation knows about this; as a result, between 70 and 80 requests come in each week for the elders to pray about. We also pray about the decisions we need to make.

"It's amazing how the more you pray about something, the more God makes your hearts one. Men who regularly pray together grow together and develop the mind of Christ."

Many Hands Make Church Work

At Servants of Christ Reformed Church, everyone works. It's a condition for membership in this Federal Way, Washington, congregation — each person agrees to join one of the church's four ministry groups:

- Administration and stewardship
- Education and worship
- Evangelism and mission
- Mercy and caring

"They become part of a resource pool," says Pastor Harold "Shorty" Brown. "The lay staff coordintor in charge of each ministry can then contact people as needed."

Ministry groups meet only twice a year, but the coordinators stay in touch with members throughout the year.

"For example, we've had four deaths in our congregation of 127 in the past two months. Nancy Brown, the coordinator for the mercy and caring ministry, discovered four people in her group who could develop a program on death and dying for our Sunday school hour."

Do people resist committing themselves to a ministry group?

"We've only had four families refuse to participate," says Brown. "I was disappointed and told them I hoped they'd reconsider, and periodically when I see them, I ask if they're ready to join up."

On the other hand, 30 regular attenders are active in the ministries but haven't joined the church yet.

Brown teaches an "Understanding Our Ministries" class that people take before joining the church.

"I keep before them the gifts that God gives," he says. "At our church we don't want any gift wasted. Everyone is here to serve others."

Basic Training for the Church Council

Being asked to run for the church council can be threatening, especially if you don't know exactly what the church council does.

That's why St. Paul's Lutheran Church in Tracy, California, recently invited several new members to attend council meetings as observers. They couldn't vote, but they were welcome to join the discussion.

"In the past two years, our church has received over 275 new members," says Pastor Michael Birnbaum. "We realized we needed to expand our board of elders from six to twelve and add another two officers to our church council. But when we contacted individuals to run for office, they weren't comfortable doing so. Some were administrators in the secular world, but they didn't know how our church was run."

As a result, Birnbaum mailed letters to nearly 20 members he felt had leadership potential, saying they were welcome to attend any church council meeting.

Ten showed up at the next meeting. Another two or three came to the subsequent meetings. They listened to the reports of committee chairmen and joined in the discussion.

"Several commented that church council meetings weren't as ominous as they'd imagined," Birnbaum reports. "We laugh together and feel free to say, 'I don't know what to do about this. What do you all think?'"

At least three have told Birnbaum they're now willing to run for church office after getting a feel for the job.

"After a term on the church council handling administrative matters, they're potential elders — those who help with pastoral tasks," says Birnbaum.

"We feel that inviting observers to the council is a

useful tool in recruiting officers and easing the transition into leadership."

How to Find (and Keep) a Chairperson

Promise them anything — so long as they take the job.

That's the approach of too many churches when recruiting committee heads, says Harvey D. Moore, minister of First Christian Church in Liberal, Kansas. It doesn't work, for two reasons: either the person is wise to the charade and refuses, or else the person agrees to serve — and soon gets overwhelmed by the job.

What's a better way? "Each summer I work out a general calendar for every committee — a folder with a page for each month," says Moore. "On each page I list the work to be done that month. I also include the relevant input from last year's committee month by month: reports, evaluations, even snapshots of certain events, suggestions for the future."

"Then, I can sit down with a prospective chairperson and say, 'Here are the specifics of what this job is all about. Here are your basic agendas for every meeting of the coming year.' Items get added or deleted along the way, of course, but the general direction is given. They know where they should be going and how to get there."

For example, the September page in the Worship Committee's folder includes, in addition to routine business, a note to begin planning for Advent. The January page calls for an evaluation of all Advent activities, a copy to go to next year's file.

"Our experience," says Moore, "is that people will accept a task much more readily when they know exactly

what they're being asked to do and have a clear idea of
how and when to do it."

Boardroom Sweetener

Board members, like siblings, often keep their
appreciation of each other to themselves. It's always easier to tangle than to affirm.

David Goodman, associate pastor of Emmanuel
Evangelical Free Church in Burbank, California, has an
antidote: a guided session of thanking God for the
strengths of others.

"I've done this with small groups, then with our
church staff of four, and it went so well we decided to try
it with our deacons," he says. "The idea is that we all
focus on one member at a time, thanking God for a specific character trait of that person, or the influence the
person carries. The format is strict conversational
prayer — brief expressions, one thought each. Individuals may pray more than once if they wish, but each
must be short and to the point.

"Then the leader says, 'Father, now we turn our attention to John (or Mary),' and the thanksgiving
continues."

The results have always been elating, says
Goodman. More than one deacon has said, "We don't
spend enough time doing things like this."

What keeps the prayers from becoming flattery?
"The leader has to introduce the exercise properly,"
Goodman advises. "I usually say, 'Scripture tells us
repeatedly to affirm one another, and tonight we'll try to
obey that. Don't make eloquent speeches; be concise.
Be truthful, but be positive as you thank God for the
other people in this room.'

"Then, as the praying begins, the leader must 'direct
the traffic' sensitively, moving from one focus to the next
at the right time.

"This will work with any group that knows one another well enough to pray intelligently. The spontaneous, infectiously supportive atmosphere really teaches people to edify each other."

A GRACEFUL GOOD-BY

A pastor and a lay leader tell how they helped each other at resignation time.

Corporations often hold exit interviews with key people who resign, but churches seldom do. Most assume it would be just too uncomfortable.

Ed Gouedy disagrees. When he left First Presbyterian Church in New Orleans, he asked for a committee of church officers who could be honest in love. They met together one evening over coffee at the home of the Ed Knights. Here's what happened.

Gouedy: The reason I called for the meeting was that I felt that we all needed to deal with our respective griefs at the death of a pastorate. Furthermore, we needed to look to the future. My wife and I were heading for a new church in Alexander City, Alabama, while these people were heading into a pastoral search. We needed to face both of these tasks constructively.

In preparation for the meeting, I drew up a handout sheet with four sections:

- What I felt good about
- What I felt bad about
- What I hoped would be different in my next church
- What I thought this church should consider as it prepared for its next pastor.

We began the evening by going over the sheet together. What little awkwardness existed was gone in five minutes. The committee affirmed my gifts in worship, preaching, and organization. I was dreading the time when the subject of home visitation came up, because I felt I hadn't done enough. They agreed things could have been better, but they disagreed with my expectations, finding them too high. The more they talked about what they thought was realistic, the more I adjusted my guidelines for the future.

They also listened well. My wife and I talked about our problems with housing — the church did not have a manse — and our struggle to cope with living in New Orleans. They not only heard what we said but began talking about ways to help the next minister discover where to live, which schools were best, and so on.

I had announced the meeting for one hour; it lasted two and a half. At the close, we all stood in a circle holding hands and praying together. Later, one of the officers told me, "When you announced your resignation, I was mad at you. I'm still upset you're leaving — but I sure am glad we had that meeting."

Knight: When our pastor called us together for an "exit interview," we had no idea that this was a novelty in church procedure. We assumed it was simply another part of his four-year campaign to bring our "old" church into the twentieth century. The idea sounded both sensible and needed.

Looking back, I realize his selection of the group was critical. We were all people who could communicate with the pastor, tolerate strong feelings, and handle divergent opinions. There were no outright enemies of the pastor — probably a wise decision.

Automatically, all of us sensed a twofold agenda: to clear the air regarding what some viewed as a self-seeking desertion, and to understand the transition better so we could convey it to various elements of the congregation. I do believe we accomplished both.

We did not spend time hashing over individual peccadilloes. Reverend Gouedy presented his sheet and also talked about his family and professional problems and aspirations. We began to see how his decision had developed out of these. The exchange was more intimate than could ever have been achieved in a congregational meeting.

We said openly that we wished he would have stayed another year or two in order to carry through the various programs he had started. But in light of his situation, we could see justification for the move. What good would his grimly sticking it out have been if it would have sapped his motivation for dedicated work? This was not a matter of blame or fault but rather the mysterious algebra of God's work in human life.

We then moved into specifics of his ministry among us. We aired things we had previously left unsaid; for example, we admitted that at times we found him abrasive and impatient. He detailed his frustration at our lack of support in some areas as well. This part of the meeting seemed to drain away feelings and led to a genuine sadness over the real issue: departure.

We ended without rancor and without any specious sense of either side winning. There was a closure as we accepted reality. We laymen saw more clearly our responsibility for our own church. A loss was commuted into a change, and a change meant opportunity for further growth — but it would not occur unless we made it happen.

In general we emerged with a better understanding that a minister's career and personal needs do not necessarily have to dovetail with a church's timetable for God's purpose to be fulfilled.

The meeting was not only successful but necessary, for those present and those to whom we spoke afterward. Post-departure acrimony has since been limited to those few who were already disaffected. A number of people continue friendly contact with the Gouedys.

Arrivals and departures, beginnings and endings, starts and finishes are an essential part of life itself. They can in no way be avoided. Thus, when a senior companion to Christian pilgrims reaches a crossroads, he should talk openly with those who can hear him, share his feelings, and pray for understanding as he turns to minister elsewhere.

FACILITIES

If the Walls Could Speak . . .

In the midst of a building program, the people of Aloha Community Baptist Church outside Portland, Oregon, got a chance to add their own personal touches.
ists had broken into the old one, taken what they wanted, and left the place in ashes.

At the point when the outside shell was restored and the roof was on, Pastor Leo Schlegel called an unusual celebration. "Bring crayons or large ink markers to church next Sunday," he announced, "and bring a favorite Bible verse to write on the interior walls and the subflooring under the altar area."

The people pored through their Bibles all week to find just the right verses. The next Sunday, they walked together into the unfinished sanctuary.

After a prayer of dedication, they sang a Scripture chorus together: "Bless the Lord, O My Soul." Pastor Schlegel read Deuteronomy 6:6-10, which says in part, "And these words, which I command thee this day, shall be in thine heart. . . . And thou shalt write them upon the posts of thy house, and on thy gates."

Then everyone was turned loose to write God's commandments and promises not only on the posts and gates, but on every wall and two-by-four within reach. (Children were advised that this was a one-time experience *never* to be repeated!)

"We visited then and walked about reading the verses," says one member, "Some had chosen personal favorites, while other had written verses appropriate to a new building. We knew our Scriptures would soon be covered with insulation and drywall, but the Word of God will always surround us."

More than one person inscribed Haggai 2:9 —
"The glory of this latter house shall be greater than of
the former, saith the Lord of hosts: and in this place will
I give peace."

52

Reported by Nyla G. Booth

BUILDING THY NEIGHBOR'S CHURCH

by Kenneth Vetters, pastor, Bartlett Chapel United Methodist Church, Danville, Indiana, with Cindy Vetters Lanning

Would church members ever volunteer to help *another* church erect its educational wing?

Before you say no, consider our situation at Bartlett Chapel, a United Methodist church of 250 members about 20 miles west of Indianapolis. Our task in the summer of 1981 was to provide approximately 6,500 square feet of space in a two-floor addition figured to cost $280,000. Estimated construction time: six months.

But that was before our people *and* fellow United Methodists from a 50-mile radius decided to give a new twist to the old barn-raising concept. The result was a wing finished in less than two months for less than $240,000.

Actually, it wasn't the first time these men and women had worked together on a construction project. Over the years, Lloyd and Marion Covey as well as other Bartlett Chapel members have joined the South Indiana Annual Conference work team that goes to Texas every winter. Each year they build a church or a parsonage for the Spanish-speaking Rio Grande Conference.

When we faced our own building project, Lloyd Covey suggested inviting the work team to consider a local project in the summer. We sent out 47 letters of invitation to those who had gone on the Texas trips. About 35 people responded. Another 20 or so of our own members signed on to help as well. Our building project was underway.

Certain work had to be hired, of course — foundation pouring, heavy steel handling, electrical and plumbing installation. But when it came to things volunteers could do, Russell Kerr, a "retired" architect and contractor from Union Chapel UMC in Indianapolis, led the group. Maynard Payne, of First UMC in Shelbyville, was the head carpenter, a sort of foreman. Lloyd Covey was Bartlett Chapel's representative, making day-to-day decisions in the name of the church. Under this leadership, the work progressed smoothly and without accidents other than bruised fingers.

One of the visiting volunteers stayed with a local family. Although we offered to keep more of the out-of-towners overnight, most of them preferred to drive home. Some volunteers worked full days, and some didn't. Farmers and others with flexible schedules came during the week, while others donated Saturdays or vacation time.

During the first few days of the project while the frame was going up, one had to lay a board down carefully, because it was almost instantly nailed down. The largest number of volunteers on any one day was 20, with fewer coming toward the end of the project when there were fewer jobs to be done.

The women of Bartlett Chapel provided daily lunch for all the workers, both volunteer and hired, from mid-August to almost the end of September. Hired laborers seemed to enjoy this time of good food and high-spirited fellowship. I couldn't begin to estimate how many gallons of coffee and especially lemonade we went through during those weeks.

But women were not confined to the kitchen. One young female volunteer from the Lawrence church helped lift up rafters and keep the supply of mortar constant to those working on the high scaffolding. Our Bartlett Chapel women did much of the time-consuming finish work such as painting and varnishing.

On weekends, the work site would resemble a county fair, with church members stopping by to check the progress as we kept working. Teenagers swept floors and nailed on roofing at the same time as retirees installed windows. How many hours were volunteered altogether? That's hard to calculate — partly because so many people worked, and partly because no one could separate the hard work from the kidding around.

I know of one hired bricklayer who ended up donating part of his hours, and others may have done this also. They gave their time because the volunteers were a loving group of people who had a lot of fun and did a lot of work, and the hired workers wanted to be a part of that.

Although some had thought 1981 was the wrong time to build, the new wing has been a tremendous experience for Bartlett Chapel because the volunteers worked together in a Christlike spirit. When I'd try to thank the visitors for their help, they'd only shrug and say that their church might need help some day.

If they do, we'll be there.

Let the Sunshine In

Question: What can a men's group do with a pile of old aluminum cans, lumber, glass, and a little black paint?

Answer: Cut the church's heating bill by more than 60 percent. At least that's what happened in the small town of Washingtonville, New York, when the men of First Presbyterian Church built their own solar heater.

Lee H. Poole, pastor, proposed the idea back in 1978, and a small three-panel unit recouped its cost the first winter. A larger eight-panel unit was installed two years ago.

Does solar heating require cutting a hole in the roof and making major changes inside? "Not at all," says Poole. "Generally, roof units are not a good idea: they're hard to service — to brush off the snow and scrape the ice — and it's hard to pump hot air *down* to where you need it.

"Our unit sits at the back of the church at ground level, with nothing but a parking lot in front of it." The panels, facing south, consist of wooden frames some 4 by 7 feet and one foot thick. The top side is two panes of glass separated by a quarter-inch space for dead air.

On the bottom rest the cans, cut in half and painted dull black. Insulation fills a small space behind the sheet and on all four sides. Ducts allow the building's cool air to enter the base of the panels, where it is heated to 140 degrees. Fans draw the heated air out through another duct at the top and distribute it throughout the building. A thermostat below is linked to a thermo-coupler atop the unit to activate the fans when the sun appears.

"The slant of the panels is determined by how far north you are," Poole adds. "Obviously, this is a subsidy system — it can't do the whole job. But there are many winter weekdays that our oil furnace never kicks on; the solar unit warms the building enough to keep pipes from freezing. Our total savings in 1981 was around $3,700 of the $5,800 we would have paid for oil."

Scale drawings and further information are available for $1 from First Presbyterian Church, Goshen Ave., Washingtonville, NY 10992.
Reported by Ernestine Gravley

HOW ONE CHURCH CONSERVES ENERGY

by Carol B. Smith, Madison, Wisconsin

In 1977 the energy crisis became real for Trinity Lutheran Church in Madison, Wisconsin, when members learned their utility bills could total one million dollars during the next twenty-two years.

"That realization became a spur to doing something," said the pastor of the congregation at the time. There were many possibilities for action: installation of ceiling fans; insulation of walls, windows, boilers, hot water heaters, and ceilings; use of controlled thermostats, some with timers attached; lowered ceilings; purchase of new, more efficient furnaces or conversion from oil to gas heat; better caulking and weatherstripping; addition of storm windows; and construction of entry vestibules for wind protection. Changes in schedule were also listed among conservation measures: meetings held in homes during the week; meetings held at church on the same night of the week; worship held in the basement during the coldest weather; and entrances locked on unprotected sides of the buildings in winter.

Trinity Lutheran, with a congregation of over 2,000 and a very large, very inefficient building, decided on a three-phase program. Phase one for conserving energy included new storm windows, a new boiler pump, and timers on thermostats. But the major expenditure was for insulation and re-roofing of the sanctuary and education buildings. The projects were based on a study of specific needs, and the pastor admits many were costly. "We had a special fund drive and raised our $50,000 goal in eight months. We're not a congregation renowned for exceptional generosity; we simply realized the money would be spent one way or another. People will respond to the cost of conserving," he said. "The beauty of money spent like this is it's like compound interest. Each year you save more."

"Over half of the money ($29,000) went for the roof and insulation work," said the current chairman of the property management commission of Trinity (also a home repairs contractor). "The ceiling was our main loss of heat. An estimate of six years to complete recovery of our cost is conservative."

Phase two began in 1980. All work on this phase was done in the absence of a pastor. Again, the cost of $15,000 was met by a fund drive that asked members for a six-month pledge.

Most aspects of phase two were aesthetic improvements to the altar area. But as part of that, the 260 seventy-five watt bulbs on the sanctuary valance were replaced with four-foot, dimmable fluorescent fixtures. "We will cut down the operating costs of those lights by three-fourths and get twice the light." Total cost was $4,100. Dimmable fluorescents are about one-third more than regular fluorescents, but they expect full recovery of cost in three years' savings on electricity.

Phase three, now in progress, involves two unique projects and again seeks a $15,000 total in special pledges from members. The first project involves repairs to the washrooms.

Another project is for a courtyard that is completely enclosed by the sanctuary wall on one side and the educational unit walls on three other sides. The cost of putting storms on the nineteen windows there would have been $7,000. Instead, Trinity will roof the courtyard and include vents and skylights, thus warming the space with solar heat in winter and venting hot air in summer. Total cost will be $9,000 with full recovery in four to five years.

"The project was not feasible before," said the chairman.

"Now with energy costs so high, it becomes feasible to do what you've never considered before."

Volunteers were not used to *complete* many of these projects; most were just too technical for that. But volunteers did manage the entire program and helped with renovations in a number of ways:

- Weatherstripping is done every year by volunteers.
- Volunteers managed the three fund-raising efforts.
- Small carpentry work and cabinet making were contracted to members on a "time and materials basis." Though not strictly volunteer work, the individuals gave a lot of quality time for the money they charged.
- Painting, cleaning, and moving furnishings were done by volunteers.
- A renovating committee went over the whole church and decided what projects to undertake in each phase. Work was overseen and expedited by volunteers on a property management committee.

The awareness for energy conservation that began at Trinity and grew in the Southern Wisconsin American Lutheran churches in the late seventies has also been shared with the Lutheran church nationwide. At its 1978 general convention, the American Lutheran Chruch was asked to address the energy problem. A task force was appointed, and by 1980, they had:

- made available two books on energy conservation, *The Energy Efficient Church* and *Total Energy Management,* to the 4,800 congregations.
- developed a model for workshops on energy conservation for use by groups of congregations.
- published an energy guide for congregations.
- encouraged energy conservation measures, including audits, at the church's private colleges, seminaries, camps, and related institutions.
- sought and shared information from its congregations.

In the final analysis, energy awareness is not just a matter

of financial necessity. It's a question of stewardship. "We saw
our situation as a churchwide issue," said the former pastor
of Trinity Lutheran. "If we are not efficient, that hits at the
thrust of the gospel. Many dollars that should be spent on
missions are spent on energy instead."

One layman, an electrician, said, "People know energy
will cost more. This means people will have to conserve *and*
give more, so that money for benevolence is not used to pay
the utilities."

Cheap Space Fast

David Wong and the Chinese Alliance Church of Wheaton, Illinois, recently acquired a worship facility for a miserly $13.50 per square foot. And they were able to occupy within a matter of weeks.

How? They found a school district ready to sell a three-unit mobile classroom cluster.

"We had bought a piece of property, but when our building committee started to meet with contractors, we realized we just couldn't afford to build," says Wong. "Then another pastor mentioned the idea of converting portable classrooms.

"We actually bought the units for just $500 apiece, complete with air conditioning, electric heat, overhead lighting, and washrooms. By the time we finished moving and remodeling the units and paying the architect, we had spent an affordable $35,000. And we can accommodate over 200 worshipers."

Other school systems have been known to *give* away mobile units no longer needed.

"Now we're really bringing prayers back into the classroom," Wong adds with a grin.

Free Classroom Space — and a Crowd to Fill It

Pastor James Schackel has faced the same pair of problems in two successive parishes: (1) no space in which to start a new adult Bible class and thereby relieve crowding in the existing class; (2) a contingent of members who skip class in favor of stopping by a restaurant en route to church.

He's solved both problems at once by simply taking the Bible study to the restaurant.

"When I was at Redeemer Lutheran in Salem, Oregon," relates, "there was a restaurant only two blocks from the church. I talked the manager into letting us put a class in his meeting room. People came, ordered from the menu, socialized a bit, and then we began our discussion of a book such as Keith Miller's *Habitation of Dragons*."

"Here at Zion Lutheran" (Montrose, Colorado) "we've done the same thing in a restuarant, using an upstairs area while the general public eats downstairs. Some people have just coffee, or coffee and a sweet roll, while others order a full breakfast. We're currently going through *Your God Is Too Small* by J. B. Phillips."

The important thing is that a restaurant class appeals to a different kind of individual, one who probably is not active in the usual Sunday morning class anyway. "Our main class maybe lost a few in the beginning," says Schackel, "but it built right back up again. In the meantime, the restaurant class is drawing 12 to 20 people."

Marjorie Ferrin, who with her husband, Paul, taught a restaurant class in San Jose, California, for six years, is another firm believer in the concept. Now that Bethel Church has completed larger facilites, her class had moved back to the church property, "but some of our people still wish we'd go back to the restaurant," she admits. "Two other groups — a college class and a single-adult class — are still meeting in restaurants, and I doubt if the single adults will ever move. They really do prefer that atmosphere."

The restaurant where the Ferrins taught was not open at the hour their class met, but the management agreed to provide coffee, rolls, and a waitress for approximately $1.35 per person. Class offerings covered the cost.

Hints for a restaurant teacher: Keep one eye on the clock. Don't let the hour evaporate into extended chit-chat; start the presentation at a given time even if food is still being served. People can chew and listen at the same time.

Also, be diligent to stop on time, allowing enough minutes for travel to the morning service.

The Last Come First

Throughout the week the five pastors of First Baptist Church, Monroe, Louisiana, enjoy reserved parking spaces close to an entrance. But on Sundays, they take their chances with the rest of the 800 worshipers in order to give visitors a break.

Portable signs that say "Reserved for visitors" are rolled out to hold the five pastoral spots and five others for late-arriving newcomers.

"We're a downtown church," explains Jerry Squyres, minister of education, "and parking is limited. It's been our experience that most visitors arrive just in time for church or perhaps even a little late. If they have to search very long for a parking place, they enter the service even later; this causes embarrassment — and a reluctance to return."

But thanks to the signs, visitors can park right beside the covered walk that leads to the educational building. They know even before they step inside that the church has thought about their needs.

Shuttle Parking: Yes, It's Feasible

If a church is out of parking space and can't buy any more, the only solution is to move, right?

Wrong. At least some churches are proving that members *can* be talked into a shuttle system. One of the largest is Los Gatos Christian Church in California, where almost half the Sunday morning crowd parks at outlying shopping centers or schools and rides church-provided buses the rest of the way.

This is a megachurch — three morning services that draw a total of 4,300. But the church campus has only 580 parking spaces, and the city won't allow more. About 100 close-in spaces are reserved for first- and second-time visitors. The other 480 fill up quickly. Meanwhile, a fleet of 12 buses — most owned by the church, some rented — circulate continually from 7:30 A.M. to 1:00 P.M., transporting 2,000 people each week.

"Many actually find the buses more convenient," says Carl Palmer, outreach pastor. "Others do it out of concern to minister to visitors, not wanting to clog the lots we have." Still others say they enjoy the fellowship on the bus, since they see many of the same riders each week.

In the beginning, the shuttle system was given high publicity at the church, with flyers on all windshields showing a map of the remote lots and pick-up times. By now, people have accepted shuttling as a fact of life. And the church continues to grow.

Reported by Harold Olsen

HOW WE DETHRONED EDIFICE REX

by Frank Tillapaugh, pastor, Bear Valley Baptist Church, Denver, Colorado, with Marshall Shelley

It was a nice problem to have, but that didn't make finding a solution any easier. In five years, our church had grown from 83 to over 400. The sanctuary could seat 250, and even with double services, we were uncomfortably crowded.

The building had been built with an eye toward saving money, but now we were paying the price. Walls curved where they weren't supposed to, rest rooms were tiny, and the nursery was hopelessly overcrowded.

Nor did we have room to expand. Bear Valley owned less than two acres, and with churches on both sides in an otherwise residential area, street parking on Sunday morning was almost as competitive as at Mile High Stadium on Sunday afternoon. Even if we enlarged the sanctuary to its maximum, our present location would limit the size of a congregation to 300.

Normal procedure for growing churches, of course, is to fill the buildings to "capacity," then move to the edge of the city and erect a larger building. We were convinced our growth would explode if only we had facilities big enough to service everyone. A bigger and better location seemed the natural move.

But many of us were uneasy about moving deeper into both suburbia and debt.

We didn't want to become part of the "white flight" to the outskirts when the city needs more strong churches to stay.

We also realized that complex buildings can produce a building complex. When 50 percent or more of the church budget goes into mortgages, utilities, and maintenance, the people become servants of the building. Options for creatively reaching the world outside the church fortress are reduced. When needed staff or programs can't be added because payments on a building that's used two hours a week are too steep, the building has set the priorities of the church.

Our associate pastor, Roger Thompson, was fond of quoting an old New England proverb:

Fix it up, wear it out.
Make it do, or do without.

An accomplished carpenter and furniture maker, Roger thought our present building could be adapted to keep the ministry growing.

"Everything I've ever had has been used," Roger said, "whether it was a car or a TV set. I was taught to fix it up and make it work again. I'd rather do that than get something new."

Roger's attitude was contagious. Rather than move out and build a spacious cathedral, the church decided to stay put and trust our creativity to find ways to expand the ministry.

An extensive remodeling job enlarged the nursery, improved the rest rooms, transformed several small classrooms into a large multipurpose room with movable partitions, and expanded the sanctuary seating capacity to 300.

But the real transformation was in the attitudes of the people. When churches opt for the amphitheater approach to ministry, people tend to get smaller as the buildings get larger. We found the converse was also true, at least for us. When we made a conscious decision to downplay the importance of the building, people felt like their creativity had been given a vote of confidence.

Lay people began to understand that the Christian life

isn't lived within the walls of the church. They began to become not members of "God's house," but "God's hosts" in an inhospitable world. They were forced to see that ministries can't be based inside the church fortress — there simply wasn't room. The only option was creative decentralization.

Our singles ministry began a Sunday breakfast in a nearby restaurant. People began ministering to international students on local college campuses, and to street people in a rented coffee house, and to one another in home Bible studies.

We still had a problem with Sunday worship. Where could we pack the people? Again, creative decentralization was our only choice.

Some people assume that for the Body to be the Body, everyone must meet together at one time. We challenged that assumption. Instead of fatter body cells, why not multiply the cells?

While many churches have offered multiple services, we took the next logical step — multiple congregations, each with a different flavor.

We started a 5:15 P.M. congregation in the remodeled multipurpose room. Instead of offering a clone of the morning congregation, we wanted to offer a true choice, to attract a different set of people. So 5:15 was informal — a coffee break punctuated the service so people could get acquainted. People from our street ministry, in their jeans and T-shirts, were welcomed. There was time for sharing.

Since setting up a whole new bureaucracy for an embryonic congregation is exhausting and often fatal, we didn't have a choir, Sunday school, or committees. A nursery and informal growth groups during the week were the only auxiliary ministries for 5:15.

For a while, 5:15 relieved attendance pressure on 11:15, but before long, the morning service was overcrowded again. What next? We began an 8:00 A.M. congregation with a different pastor in charge. This new congregation developed a personality all its own — a blend of traditional and informal, and using quite a bit of intergenerational activities.

Currently five congregations, totaling over 1,000 people, meet in Bear Valley's modest facility that seats 300. And a mission church of about 70 has been started on East Colfax in Denver's inner city. Besides the pastor of the mission church, three different pastors lead the various congregations in the mother church.

How do we know we're still one church? People inter-mingle every week in the outreach ministries, which draw from all the congregations. We also see one another at the 7:00 P.M. Sunday fellowship hour — not a preaching service, but a mix of musical events, film series, and assorted work-shops. And of course, we're united structurally — one deacon board, one budget, common business meetings.

Looking back, that decision in 1976 to stay put was the best we could have made. Modest facilities help a church retain the advantages of a small church while enjoying the re-sources of a big church.

Modest facilities help people stay visible. If no congrega-tion can grow over 300, those 300 faces grow more familiar.

A small facility is also less intimidating. A junior higher can sing in a smaller sanctuary more easily than in a cathedral. The pastor is more approachable if he preaches from merely a few feet away than if he mounts a stage to thunder to the masses. Small facilities keep things up close and personal.

People also are forced to stay active. More congregations demand more lay involvement as well as a bigger need to de-velop more pastoral leadership. The bigger the church, the more potential for spectators.

Finally, modest facilities allow the church to spend more money on people. American auto makers are in trouble because they failed to predict in time the demand for small, economical cars. American churches will soon face the same predicament if they insist on constructing buildings large enough to seat everyone at once. Land, building materials, in-terest rates, and inflation can strangle a church budget.

Some experts predict utility bills soon will equal the mortgage payment.

This is one reason why, by comparison, parachurch organizations seem so effective. A smaller percentage of their funds are required for buildings. More funds are used for staff involved directly with people ministries. Churches can certainly move this direction.

There's something exciting about ministering to 1,000 people while maintaining a building for 300 — especially when we know that we can at least double our number in the same facility. Plus, we can keep growing by planting churches elsewhere.

Small facilities don't stop a church from having a major ministry. They just make you take the creative, scenic route to get there.

TWO CHURCHES IN ONE BUILDING — IT WORKS

by Lane A. Fusilier, pastor, Fellowship Bible Church, Waco, Texas

We were desperate. No more chairs could be squeezed into the small schoolroom where we were meeting. The private school had no larger rooms suitable for worship, and the local public school district discouraged church rentals. The consistent growth of our church's first year was being choked, and every option we investigated was either inappropriate or too expensive.

Fellowship Bible Church of Waco was organized in the fall of 1978. We met in a home for several months, until rapid growth forced us to lease space in the private school. Our children's classes and adult Sunday school had plenty of space, but the largest room that could be used for worship held just under 100 people. We used what was available as creatively as we could and began our search for new facilities.

Several members visited every conceivable type of building. We discovered a church building for sale in an older section of town. We were willing to meet there but were wary of the price and the remodeling needs. Another building for sale was located through a realtor — commercial space in an abandoned downtown shopping district. Even that radical opportunity was pursued and examined closely before we came to the same conclusion: too much money for both purchase and remodeling. Meanwhile, the longer we looked for another facility, the greater the need became.

One of our men worked with a member of the local Seventh-day Adventist church. While discussing our problem, the two hit upon the possibility of renting the SDA building on Sundays.

Several men took the idea to the SDA pastor, Jim Graves. After exploring our doctrinal position and what kinds of building uses we sought, Pastor Graves consulted with his church board and subsequently offered us the use of their building for $500 a month. That was a fair price, but higher than we felt we could handle on a monthly basis. The church graciously agreed to start our rent at about what we were then paying to use the private school. We gradually increased our rent on a regular basis until we met their income request. We have the facility each Sunday morning and, for a small additional fee, the opportunity to use it Sunday evening or most any other evening when it is not in use. Each extra payment covers the cost of utilities.

A typical week in the life of Fellowship Bible Church begins with Sunday morning worship and Sunday school at the Adventist building. About once a week, groups of four or five families meet together in Fellowship Families, a variation of the mini-church concept. The idea works especially well for our church because it fills our need for edification without requiring a large building. Special events, such as Christmas services or missionary engagements, are occasionally held in the SDA building on Sunday evenings. We enjoy celebrating baptisms at Lake Waco and include Communion with the public profession of faith, then have a picnic together. (An option in inclement weather is to use the SDA baptisty during our morning worship hour.) One Thanksgiving service was celebrated at a home restored by the historical society and available for public rental. All of these services might have been held at the Adventist building, but we have found that a variety of environments has underlined the significance of each service for our members.

The working relationship between our two churches could hardly be better. We have our own storage areas for, among other things, our own hymnals. We have worked out a system to guarantee building security and care of equipment just as we would for our own building.

Communication between the churches has been aided by the regular presence of Earl Heslop, a retired Adventist deacon who voluntarily comes most Sunday mornings and attends all of our special functions. By that effort, he has smoothed the relationship, keeping us aware of potential difficulties and helping us gain maximum use of the building and its furnishings.

Obviously we have to work at establishing a clear identity in the community, explaining that we're a separate church that "meets in the Adventist building on Highway 6." It also took us a while to catch on to the Adventist view of caffeine drinks and stop leaving our coffee cups around after the fellowship hour! But these adjustments are well worth the savings; building and maintaining a new structure in the present economy would be prohibitive for us.

Pastor Graves agrees that the finances are a priority; our rental fees help them with their utility bills, perhaps the most important benefit. However, he adds that "the idea of helping another church" is of great importance, too. Adventist churches often rent other churches as they are getting started, he notes, so they feel it's their privilege to return the favor.

We have just begun our third year of sharing the SDA building. We consider it a privilege to help maximize its use and do not expect to leave until growth demands more space. Perhaps the final argument comes from Jim Graves, when asked what his church would do if Fellowship Bible moved to another facility: "We'd look for another church to use our building!"

THE GOSPEL GOES DOWNTOWN

by Daryl Fenton, associate pastor, Loop Evangelical Free Church, Chicago

I unlock the doors of the old building like I have a thousand other days. The night crew has gone. They have removed the traces of 4,000 people who passed through these oak-paneled rooms yesterday. The aroma of Wiener schnitzel and tobacco, coffee and beer has largely been replaced by the smell of wood polish and glass cleaner. The silence is heavy in contrast to the symphony of china cups and saucers, glasses and ice that accompany waiters with 30 different accents who play these halls six days a week. It's Sunday, and The Berghoff Restaurant is closed.

Passersby look hopefully at me, key in hand. I explain, "No, the restaurant won't be open today, but we'll be having a church service soon. You're welcome to join us."

I've worked at the Berghoff, a half block off famous State Street for 12 years. As each year passed, I became increasingly aware of my limited ability to meet the needs of the people with whom I rubbed shoulders each day. Christian friends, including Craig Burton (now our pastor), felt that same immediacy of need throughout all of downtown Chicago. So when I asked the Berghoff family if we could use their landmark building for a church, I witnessed a miracle in their wholehearted response.

The Burtons were ready to move to the city and take the risk of starting a new work. So we moved a few tables, told a few people, prayed a great deal — and Loop Evangelical Free Church was born.

Why start a church in the heart of Chicago's business district? Ten thousand people moved here to *live* during the last several years. Thirty thousand more residents are expected within the next five years. Tens of thousands work here each day. There aren't enough churches to meet a challenge this large. These people live out their lives, as do all city dwellers, in an intense, intemperate environment. The need for proclaiming and living a sin-deflating gospel in an atmosphere of care and warmth is great.

For that reason, each Sunday morning finds us turning a dining room into a sanctuary. The entrance on the lower level becomes a nursery. Just around the corner, past the display table, you'll find the primary class. We roll the stage into the large west dining room and put it under the mirror. A music stand substitutes for a pulpit. Guitars, banjos, flutes and an electric piano stand in for more traditional instruments. Somehow, in the inimitable way the Holy Spirit always works, when we're all done it feels like a church. Even the stained-glass windows, with their beer steins and grapevine designs, lend pastel hues to the transformation.

The people will be coming soon. The core group of committed Christians who began this adventure with us will arrive, some from forty miles away. There will also be those who week by week have joined us. City people for the most part, but not as many from the nieghborhood as we first expected, they have enlarged Loop Church to about 60 people. Many are Christians, but more and more come who need Christ's love. Our reason for existing is beginning to emerge.

The Berghoff is proving uniquely appropriate for the job God wanted done. Its familiar name and location simplify directions to Loop Church. The informal atmosphere, with its patina of old Chicago, provides a nonthreatening place for people unaccustomed, or even hostile, to church. The solid oak tables automatically promote a sense of warmth and intimacy that greatly enhances a stranger's ability to worship.

Because we can use The Berghoff only on Sunday, small

groups must meet in homes. The place compels us to be the kind of church Craig believes we should be — a "go" church. We are forced to carry our faith and our church life into the various worlds in which we live. We don't have a place where all the activities of the church can take place. Therefore we must take those activities to the places we have.

The informality of the surroundings spills over into the Sunday morning format. Worship and instruction precede a coffee break. The break, made possible by gleaming stainless steel urns, introduces a discussion time. Small groups, using questions coordinated with the sermon, wrestle through incorporating a specific biblical principle into their lives. Tables make for good and comfortable discussions. Topics like "making room in your schedule for prayer" and "how to live in the Kingdom of God if you're a Democrat" bring those discussions to life.

By using a facility that isn't always a church, we have "invited" people into our church who might not otherwise come. We feel a responsibility to make cultural, though not theological, adjustments for those people. In a limited and modest way, we try to look at the culture of the neighborhood around us as missionaries would see it. We adapt as many of our church forms as we can and explain what we can't adjust.

We are rank amateurs, of course, but the learning process has been exhilarating. The greatest beneficiaries have turned out to be those of us in the church who have been Christians for some time. Rethinking and reworking the ways in which we express our faith has forced us to deal very seriously with our own Christianity.

Worshiping at our church in a restaurant produces one other benefit. We feel it most when a potential customer finds the restaurant closed but decides to stay and join us for church. There is a special pleasure in seeing the Holy Spirit transform Chicago's most famous saloon into a fit place for the King of Heaven.

In Case of Unholy Smoke

Should churches go to the bother of fire drills? Although virtually none do, the idea has its merits. In the late 1950s, Living Faith Baptist Church in Nashville had drills every six weeks or so — and was glad it did the morning the small wooden structure caught fire in the middle of Sunday school. Teachers tested the hallway doors, found them hot, and led the children out the windows as planned.

"My children and I escaped safely, along with everybody else," says Ruby White, third-grade teacher as well as mother of five in the Sunday school. "We'd practiced getting out of the building any number of times, and all of a sudden the need was real."

Children and teens, being accustomed to fire drills in school, had learned to take the drills in stride once they became a regular part of Sunday morning. Teachers found them disruptive at first but soon managed to plan around them.

"I always knew several days in advance when we'd have one and what time," says White. "Then I'd take a good look at my lesson plans for that week. I could usually time it so the drill would disrupt an activity, not a story or prayer time. We got to where the whole thing took no more than five minutes.

"Sure it was extra work for us teachers — but wasn't it worth it?" The church burned to the ground, but no one was hurt.

Reported by Mary Louise Kitsen

WHEN THE CHURCH BURNS DOWN

*by David S. Swift, Arlington Heights Evangelical Free Church,
Arlington Heights, Illinois*

At 5:30 on Saturday morning, December 11, 1982, a
passing patrolman spotted flames shooting from the roof of
Arlington Heights (Ill.) Evangelical Free Church. Within
minutes, fire fighters were dragging hoses into the sanctuary
to combat the flames and 400-degree heat. Other firemen
scrambled to punch vent holes in the roof.

By the time the fire was brought under control, the
$150,000 pipe organ was destroyed, the pews were charred,
the electrical control boards melted into the bricks, and the
plastic globes on the chandeliers had dripped to the floor. Our
vaulted, 600-seat sanctuary was ravaged, the stained-glass
windows blackened. The offices and educational wing suffered
smoke damage.

Fire trucks were still on the scene as the church board
convened in the garage, the only place not filled with smoke.
Trying to shake the trauma, they wrestled with a double crisis: within eight hours, hundreds would begin arriving for the
first of four very popular Christmas concerts, and by Sunday morning, 1,200 faithful would need a place to worship.

What do you do first? This was no time to consult the
minutes for past policy. Quickly the board arranged to use
nearby Hersey High School for Sunday services, and the
Saturday concerts were swtiched to Sunday evening in the
school auditorium.

In one short week, the church learned volumes about crisis management. Associate Pastor Dave Wardle shares the lessons learned:

1. *Concentrate on immediate needs and issues.* Keep asking, "What do we need to do *now?*" and then do it.

2. *Establish clear lines of authority.* Let everyone know who is in charge of specific areas such as cleanup, security, and communications. "We tried to make one man primarily responsible for investigations by fire and insurance officials," says Wardle.

3. *Emphasize accountability.* The need for accountability wasn't apparent at first. On the morning of the fire, volunteers showed up with shovels, buckets, and mops to clear the rubble outside and remove the smoke stains inside. No one wasted time asking, "Who's in charge here?" The cleanup task was obvious, and they went to it.

In the days that followed, however, the need for accountability became obvious. People began carrying home individual items for cleaning and restoration. One family even dismantled the grand piano, hauled it home, and had experts repair the works while they restored the wood. Others took light fixtures or nursery toys. They didn't realize the insurance adjuster needed to see the damage before it was lovingly eradicated.

Striving for a balance between tight control and an atmosphere of spontaneity, we took steps to document everything. We told all volunteers: "If you want to take it home for fixing and cleaning, take pictures first. Then sign it out. It'll pay when the insurance company wants to settle."

4. *Brace yourself for the scavengers.* Within the first five days, we had several strangers poking through the rubble. One man asked if he could have a damaged pew. He wanted to use it as a counter top.

These people have to be told no — at least until the insurance company lists a complete inventory of damaged property and gives you a release to remove the items. Then you can do with them what you want.

5. *Establish security.* A related problem: many scavengers and curiosity seekers will come by to gawk or carry off a souvenir. We had to make sure no one entered the sanctuary because the fire had weakened the structure, and it was a "hard hat" area.

We didn't have to worry about our own people, but we made all outsiders wanting access to the area sign in, giving name, purpose, time in, and time out. It sounds hard-nosed, but it's a common practice in business. The insurance adjuster insisted on it.

6. *Get ready for the ambulance chasers.* Just after the fire, a man called wanting the pastor's home number. He refused to tell why, insisting it was extremely urgent. He turned out to be a carpet salesman. The office staff needs to be just as resistant to giving out names and numbers as the callers are aggressive in demanding them.

7. *Deal with contractors in writing.* Tell even the contractors you know: "Send us a letter. Our building committee will get back to you." Phone calls and visits drain your energy and divert you from your immediate concerns.

8. *Record all offers of help.* From the beginning, parishioners were a wealth of expertise and resources, but when special needs arose, leaders couldn't remember everyone who had volunteered. They learned to keep a pad by the phone, and soon they had several pages of names, numbers, and offers.

One woman revealed she had a typesetting business in her basement, and she was able to produce bulletin inserts for Sunday morning.

9. *Use your own people.* This was a real eye opener. At the outset, the congregation tackled every dirty job imaginable. By Monday, a professional cleaning service was there with their fire cleanup unit. But the parishioners were still coming, not thinking that the insurance would pay professionals to do everything.

One man arrived determined to clean the baked-on smoke stain from borrowed stage lights. When a leader told him, "Forget it — the service will do it," the man was deflated, having psyched himself up to do this miserable job for God.

"We saw what was happening," says Wardle, "and realized two significant facts. First, the insurance would also pay our people to clean. Learning that, we asked volunteers to document the number of hours spent working. That money would go to the church to cover uninsured losses."
However, insurance pays more for work done by professionals.

"Second, although the professionals could probably do it better, there was no way to calculate the blessing people received from such a sacrificial labor of love." Wardle said allowing people to restore their own church helps revolutionize their commitment to the body.

But some jobs were best done by the pros. While the initial surge of volunteers faded as the crisis excitement waned, the pros kept plugging along because they were on the payroll.

10. Communicate, communicate. The 1,200 who attend Sunday morning are scattered throughout many suburbs. The staff discovered that many were still not hearing all the schedule changes, though annoucnements ran in many local papers. So a bulletin insert asked, "What papers do you read?"

Also, on the morning of the fire, the office was deluged with calls. Someone thought to bring in a telephone-answering machine, which gave a recorded announcement. It continued to be used for some time to convey schedule changes.

11. Remember warm fuzzies. Days off were impossible, and by the end of the first week, the office and pastoral staff were exhausted. That's when a huge floral arrangement arrived. The little card read: "To the staff from the board. Hang in there, we're praying for you." Wardle said, "I can't tell you how much that revived our spirits."

Trustee Fred Wubs had two suggestions on what to do *before* the church burns down.

- Make sure you are fully insured. Spend the extra

money and effort to determine actual replacement cost. Don't guess at it.

- Make sure a fire alarm is mounted outside the building for neighbors to hear. Also, seriously consider one of several reporting systems. One is a smoke detector that activates an automatic dialer, which calls the fire department and several church leaders with a recorded message saying a fire has been detected. Another type is a smoke/heat detector that alerts a commercial security service.

Our church decided to hook up directly to the fire department. The monthly charge may seem expensive, but it's cheap considering the damage it prevents by early detection. As one fireman said, "The only churches with an adequate alarm system are those that have already had a fire."

MATERIALS
AND EQUIPMENT

Library Alive

What motivates a congregation with an adult
membership of 504 to check out about a hundred books
every Sunday, bringing the total to almost 6,000 for
the year?

Mrs. Marjorie Zimmerman, of MacArthur Park
Evangelical Lutheran Church in San Antonio, gives
primary credit to the high priority Pastor George
Schwanenberg gives to reading. This is evident in a number of ways.

1. An annual library budget in the area of $2,500.

2. The pastor refers frequently to books and
encourages people to read.

3. Library location is given primary consideration.
In the church's first education unit, the library had the
prime position. In 1980 when the congregation built
an additional educational unit, they planned it with the
library in the center. The large hallway leading from
the old library (still used for family and children's books)
to the new is utilized as a promotional area. Both sides
of the hallway are lined with shelves displaying books.
These books are changed frequently.

The entrance to the new library unit is a large foyer-
type room with two sides of glass with double doors,
making the library both visible and easily accessible to
all. This section contains a desk and comfortable chairs.
One entire wall is lined with over 600 cassettes (*not*
the pastor's sermons). Records and magazines are also
available for check-out.

The core of the new library unit (and its largest
room) is the reference room with commentaries and
study help books. Two round reading tables invite
people to use this room.

To reach the fireside room, where Bible studies are held and youth meet, one must pass through the youth books area.

4. A lively four-page brochure about the library is included monthly in the church's newsletter.

5. A volunteer plans three reading charts a year to show who is reading the most.

6. An expensive book is purchased each year in honor of new members, who then autograph it. The same is done for graduates.

7. Care is given to stock the library with materials that speak to people's felt needs.

The library is now in the process of developing a good, extensive file in clippings and pamphlets.

While Zimmerman credits the pastor with the success of the library, he is quick to note that her enthusiasm and belief in the importance of what she is doing overflows and catches fire with others.

Reported by Mildred Tengbom

The Little Library That Could

Book lovers at the small military chapel at Fort Allen in Puerto Rico were determined to encourage reading despite their size. Beginning with a few dozen books, mostly paperback, they began setting up a book table for the after-service fellowship periods. A simple paper and pencil checkout system was used to keep track of the books.

As people began using them, donations of additional books and money began trickling in. Soon, two tables were needed, and only a portion of the books could be displayed each Sunday. "That way people didn't get tired of seeing the same old titles every week," says Linda Dottery. The displayed books were varied according to seasonal, Sunday school, and sermon emphases.

Chaplain M. L. Trawick promoted the book table from the pulpit and in the bulletin and chapel newsletter. In addition, a knowledgeable person or two circulated around the tables recommending titles and giving brief comments on some of the books. Sunday school teachers recommended titles or took a few to their classrooms for checkout. "The closer we got the books to the people, the more successful we were in circulating them," Wanda Trawick comments. "Most people won't go out of their way to obtain a book."

Her conclusion: "Taking the books to the people is more effective than inviting them to the books!"

Stocking the Stacks

Church librarians sometimes don't know whether to smile or cry at the obsolete books people donate. The library committee at Evangel Baptist Church, Wheaton, Illinois, however, has found a way to get donations it wants.

Late in the spring each year, a Sunday evening service is declared "Library Night." A guest author or editor is invited to give an emphasis on reading. Following the service, while refreshments are served, people peruse an assortment of preselected books, records, and tapes the committee has gotten on consignment from a nearby Christian bookstore.

"The idea is that you buy one of the items you like — and give it to the church library," explains Don Day, chairman of the Christian education board. "Book donors fill out a book plate on the spot to be placed inside the front cover, and they also get the privilege of being the first to check the book out."

Thus the library nets two or three dozen books in a single night without having to purchase them out of budgeted funds. And they're books the librarians really wanted in the first place.

"Our family has been active in six different churches over the years," says Day, "and this is the best church library I've ever seen. Ruth Skanse and her committee pay close attention to the interests of all ages, so that young people use the resources a great deal. The once-a-year Library Night keeps us all aware of what's available."

Solving the Storage Headache

Whoever has enough storage space? The problem is compounded if the church meets in rented facilities. Anyone who has lugged hymn books or teaching supplies in cardboard boxes for very many weeks knows the frustration.

After two years of hauling, Milton Baptist Church in Ontario finally took action. "We got permission from the landlord to keep a large cupboard on wheels in an equipment locker beside the auditorium," Pastor Kelvin Mutter explains. "One of our men designed the trolley and another built it."

The cart is about three feet high, four feet long, and three feet wide, with gull-wing doors that lift up. On the inside of one door is a bulletin board; on the other is a chalkboard.

Running lengthwise through the middle is a long compartment for nursery equipment. Both outsides have shelving for 120 hymnals plus other resources. All three doors have locks.

"Now instead of carrying endless armloads from our cars," says the pastor, "we simply roll out our invention, unlock it, and have everything we need to func-

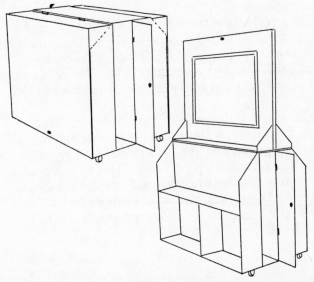

tion. It has greatly simplified the task of setting up and putting away." No wonder it has gained the nickname "The Jolly Trolley."

A Board to Please the Board

If you've thought about outfitting classrooms with the new "Whiteboards" that utilize dry-erase markers instead of dusty chalk, but have been put off by the price — there's a cheaper way.

"Dry-erase boards list for anywhere from $100 to $275," says Angus McDonald, pastor of the Evangelical

Free Church in Keokuk, Iowa. "We discovered that Marlite bathroom paneling at the lumber yard is the same thing — and it runs $13 a sheet! A four-by-eight panel can be cut in half to make two $6.50 boards in two different rooms."

Teachers hail the markers both for their range of colors and for the legibility gained by writing on a white instead of a dark surface. The ink dries almost instantly to a fine dust that clings to the Marlite but does not penetrate it. An eraser or cloth wipes the board clean.

McDonald adds two warnings, however: "Don't place the boards in direct sunlight — that makes any markings permanent. Also, don't use other types of markers such as felt-tip pens unless they're water-soluble.

"All our teachers who have used the boards are enthusiastic about them and would hate to go back to chalk. The only person who's happier still is the church treasurer."

An Up-the-Wall Solution

Breathes there a teacher of kindergarteners who ever had enough storage space in the classroom?

When Cheryl Kooistra taught the fours and fives at Tahlequah Bible Church in Oklahoma, she endured the usual box in the corner crammed with crayons, glue, scissors, workbooks, tape, gummed stars, and novelty seals, pawing through the mishmash each week — until she finally had a better idea.

She created what might be called a "storage banner" — a large piece of denim hung on the wall by a dowel rod, with pockets for each kind of item. "I sewed pockets according to the number and size of the things I needed to store," the teacher says, "a large, expandable pocket for books, and smaller patch pockets for other things we used in crafts." A long strip sewn at intervals made loops to hold scissors.

Kooistra, who has since moved to California, appliqued a design or word to each pocket so the children would know what belonged inside. "This not only provided some aesthetic value and organization to the room," she says, "but it made clean-up time fun, too. The children were always eager to put things in the right pocket."

THE MICROCOMPUTER: A PASTOR'S FRIEND?

by Edward A. Thomas, pastor, West Harpswell Baptist Church, South Harpswell, Maine

Yes, I know the host of concerns:

What fellowship hath light with a flickering VDT?

What concord hath our firm foundation with a floppy disk?

And what communion hath Christ with Qantel?

Will the eternal Word be mangled by word processing?

Is apostasy certain once the church, like Eve, succumbs to the lure of the Apple?

A recent booklet from my mailbox in this quiet coastal town urges me to touch not the unclean thing: "Could this be the mark of the Beast?" it thunders over a cover picture of a microchip. Unfortunately, I had already brought the unclean thing into the bosom of my pastoral study four years ago . . . and I smile as I notice that the pamphleteer found me, tucked away at the tip of this craggy 10-mile peninsula, with the help of a computer-generated mailing label. (So, incidentally, do my Christian magazines.)

To get started, I sold my coin collection back in 1978 and purchased a simple cassette-based system; and yes, my wife thought I was crazy. Although I missed the gold and silver rush, my investment has paid off rather well for both me and my small congregation.

In the beginning, I had no printer, so I used the computer with a word processing program to write and edit sermons and letters — and then copied them off the screen onto paper with my manual typewriter! Even that cumbersome method reduced my preparation time and the amount of paper I used. My cassette-based system was slow, and often while loading a program, I would spend the minutes getting something else done in the study. It was not until I expanded my system by adding more memory, a letter-quality printer, and a disk drive that it began to be truly practical.

The additional memory allowed me to write longer documents. The printer produced copy at 120 characters per second (I can hunt and peck at a rate of 2 or 3). The disk drive gave rapid access to programs and data; a program that took four minutes to load by cassette took about three seconds with a disk.

If by now you are wondering about the cost of this system, my total investment was about $2,300. This includes paper and ribbons, some programs I purchased, disks, as well as the computer and the peripherals I added. Has it been worth the investment? Yes. (Even my wife is starting to agree.)

Word processing alone has cut sermon and bulletin preparation by three hours. Those members who used to share the task of typing the weekly bulletin were impressed with the time savings and quality. Rather than having to center and type each item every time, I simply put last week's order of service on the screen, make the appropriate changes, and add the announcements. The printer spits out the master in about three minutes. As the text is printed, the program will center any lines I wish. The impact is firm and consistent, and the bulletins are the clearest they have ever been. An additional benefit is that I am able to print the words at 8.3 characters per inch rather than the normal 10 cpi. This has been a great help for parishioners with poor vision.

The physical work of writing and editing sermon outlines is no longer a chore. Deleting or adding one thought — or an entire section — is fast and easy. One Sunday morning as I was reviewing my outline, I had a late brainstorm. Sunday school was due to start in 15 minutes. I turned on the computer system, loaded the program and sermon outline, made the changes, printed a new two-page sermon outline, and walked across the street to greet the families as they arrived for Sunday school.

In addition to sermon outlines and bulletins, I now have nicely formatted letters, church reports, Sunday school material, and announcement fliers. My information letters to board members have added personal touches. "Dear Fred" is a better start than "To Advisory Board Members," and an appropriate word about each member's area of service or personal need draws the letter to a close.

I've also programmed my computer to generate word search puzzles, mazes, and attendance graphs. The children (and several adults) love the puzzles, and the ushers appreciate the charts. My head usher is now interested in learning to program the computer himself! A church survey was a breeze to analyze, and I'm developing a member/visitor data base for visitation and follow-up.

Applications exist beyond my local ministry. At a recent denominational meeting, my computer provided information about our convention's conference center. Each delegate could type in the name of his or her church, and the video monitor would display numerically and graphically how much that church had pledged, how much it had contributed to date, and how much it had left to meet its goal. In between times, the monitor flashed a graphic display of the various totals for the conference center, with a fish swimming across the screen. The terminal was often crowded throughout the meeting.

I'm currently working on some biblical adventure games (would you believe "Ark-Man"?). These will help both young and old not only learn facts about the Bible but also give them the opportunities to apply the Bible in simulated situations.

Perhaps you noticed that I have not mentioned using the

computer to keep track of the church's finances. Indeed, this is an area where the computer would do especially well. However, I'm reluctant to pursue this, because as pastor I do not want to know how much each person gives. Although the treasurer or financial secretary could enter the information, neither of them has shown any interest in updating the current system, and perhaps a congregation of our size does not need it.

This raises an important issue that tends to be forgotten even by me at times: We should never indiscriminately attempt to do everything by computer. If we do, we have ceased to use it as a tool and have become its slave. Some things can be done more efficiently and personally without computers. Even in areas where the computer can increase our efficiency, we must ask, "Is it really beneficial?" If my church had a member whose only area of service was typing the weekly bulletin, he or she should be able to serve the Lord in that way. The computer may do it faster, but that person needs the opportunity to serve much more.

In the future, I look forward to gaining access by phone line to theological libraries and informational data bases. What a great way for us pastors in remote places to keep up on what is happening in the seminaries and on the mission field. Maybe I'll even be able to take a continuing-education course or two. Don't laugh — with the many rapid developments in voice synthesizing and recognition, it should not be too long before Computer-Assisted Instruction (CAI) can verbally prompt the student and respond to the student's spoken questions. Someday you might even have access to *Leadership* on a computer data base — *Better Homes and Gardens* already distributes information this way.

Yes, I am excited about this potential for the microcomputer in the pastor's study. I also enjoy the challenge of creating and modifying programs for use in my ministry, for my three-year-old daughter, and just for fun. It has become a hobby for me, but it has also enhanced my ministry. A machine is giving me more time with people.

Another Computer?

Many more pastors would be interested in the benefits of a computer if they didn't have to
- buy the hardware,
- hire or train someone to run it, and
- solve all the changeover headaches themselves.

That fantasy has come true at the Grace Evangelical Free Church in the Twin Cities suburb of Fridley, Minnesota. "The key," says Gordon Mitchell, a trustee, "is to use home computers that members already have."

Grace Church is not especially large or wealthy. "In our membership of about 200, there are five home systems, with owners eager to use them in the service of the church. We've chosen our softward carefully, not getting too sophisticated. This assures us of back-up resources should illness strike a key member — or his computer."

Two software programs the Fridley church recommends are:
- Membership Manager (Comal Associates, Box 32415, Minneapolis, MN 55432), which not only generates mailing labels for the weekly newsletter but has the capacity to sort member names by geography. This speeds up visitation assignments and helps members learn who else in the congregation lives nearby.
- The Spreadsheet (Apple Puget Sound Library Exchange, 304 Main Ave. S., Renton, WA 98055), which produces the electronic equivalent of an accountant's scratch sheet. "Instead of meeting at the church for budget planning," says Mitchell, "we gather around a member's home computer. As we make decisions, we can easily enter the changes, analyze complex interrelationship between items, and produce instant totals."

High-Impact, Low-Cost Graphics

Like many a growing church, the Lansing (Illinois) Assembly of God had to move its morning service to a school gymnasium temporarily. One of the ways Pastor Robert L. Neuman drew worshipers' attention away from the basketball hoops and onto spiritual things was by using an overhead projector. Now, even though the congregation is back in a sanctuary, the practice continues.

"As people enter, I often have the day's sermon Scripture waiting for them on the screen. They can sit down and immediately turn their minds toward the Word." If the sermon text is not succinct (maximum for a transparency is about 50 words), Neuman may choose a correlating passage from another part of the Bible or a pertinent quotation from his study.

The Scripture is usually written inside the drawing of an open Bible or a scroll, both of which are available from Faith Venture Visuals, P. O. Box 685, Lititz, PA 17543. "I don't use the overhead every Sunday," the pastor says, " — just often enough to keep it fresh and noticed by the people. Some even mentioned to me that they use the preservice time to memorize the Scriptures that appear on the screen."

Bold red-letter banners, a foot high and 15 feet long, get everyone's attention from time to time at Whispering Lakes Community Church in Ontario, California. Assorted uses:

At Easter: "He is Risen — Hallelujah!"
At Christmas: "Joy . . . Peace . . . Light"
For giving outdoor directions: "Picnic This Way" or "Youth Car Wash $2"

The banners are commercially prepared by Computer Greetings Corp. (22019 Vanowen St., Suite K,

Canoga Park CA 91303) and can handle up to 48 characters each. Price: $7.95 including postage. The company guarantees 48-hour service from the time orders are received and will take phone orders (213-716-0666).

"We've gotten good service," reports Pastor Jon H. Allen, "and the banners have been used to great advantage. They can be read instantly from anywhere in the auditorium; they really make people take notice of our special emphasis for the day."

Banners to Be Proud Of

 What's the trick to making great banners when you're not a professional artist or calligrapher?

The overhead projector, of course. Both lettering and illustrations can be scavenged to make a master transparency. From that point, it's a simple matter to hang the banner material on a wall and project the image as large as you wish by moving the projector closer or farther away. Once the image fits properly, it can be traced onto the material.

Says Scott Denton, assistant pastor of the Community Church in Phelan, California, "I create my transparencies with rub-on letters, traced artwork — and sometimes I even photocopy an illustration straight onto the acetate. This speeds the process and improves the product.

"Odd-looking letters and bad spacing are headaches of the past once you get the 8½-by-11 image right, then blow it up."

Art for the Asking

Small drawings and designs do a lot to dress up church bulletins and newsletters. But not every church has an artist in residence; snipping and reprinting magazine graphics without permission is illegal; and books of commercial clip are expensive. Must small churches be stuck with a drab or amateurish book?

"We've discovered a free source for art," says Gary Prehn, director of Christian education at Harmony Bible Church in Danville, Iowa.

"Our local newspaper uses several clip-art books every month. As new books come in, they discard their old ones. But quite a few pieces are left that we can use."

The books contains artistic borders, alphabets, and illustrations for each season of the year.

"Contact the advertising department of your local paper," suggests Prehn. Ask if you can have the old issues of their clip-art books, and ask if you can come back every three or four months for additional books.

"We've found this gives us a steady source of excellent clip art, which improves the attractiveness of our church publications."

A Remedy for Altar Flower Saturation

"What really happened," George E. Buechner tells, "was that our church reached an altar flower saturation point. We just had too many folks who wanted to remember loved ones with altar flowers."

Solution: Use the weekly bulletin for the same purpose.

Buechner, pastor of Emmanuel Lutheran Church, Lancaster, Pennsylvania, explains, "Our church's worship and music committee encourages members to sponsor a weekly bulletin if they want to publicize a commemoration."

At the end of the year, a church volunteer mails a Bulletin Sponsorship Form to all church members. The form seeks the potential sponsor's name, address, choice of Sunday for sponsorship, wording to be used in the announcement, donation, and signature.

The cost of printing the bulletin is $7.50, but members have the option to donate more or less for this purpose.

"By the end of January," Buechner says, "most of the forms have been returned. All 52 Sundays of the coming year have a bulletin sponsor." Sometimes, he adds, there is more than one sponsor for a Sunday.

The announcement is placed in an obvious part of the bulletin and usually reads something like: TODAY'S BULLETIN IS GIVEN IN LOVING MEMORY OF JOHN SMITH BY HIS FAMILY. People who have passed away are not the only ones remembered. Some living members are honored, too. Last year, for instance, a 97-year-old parishioner was honored by her niece.

"The program gives people an ongoing way to remember loved ones," Buechner adds. "It's an additional source of income, too — without the hassle of blatant solicitation. People see this as a normal thing, a concrete and tangible project to contribute to."

By the way, flowers still find their way to the church's altar. But the saturation problem has been remedied.

Borrowers Welcome

When you need a movie projector or 40 extra folding chairs, should you ask the church down the street?

The Council of Hyde Park and Kenwood Churches

and Synagogues on Chicago's South Side has given an official answer to that question: Yes. They've even gone so far as to print a small "Directory of Resources and Sharing" that tell the 34 members who has what equipment.

Need a portable lectern? The Chicago Sinai Congregation has one.

Need choir risers? The Church of St. Thomas the Apostle can help you.

Extra tables? Hyde Park Union Church will be glad to oblige.

"Ours is one of the oldest councils of its kind in the country," says Ilene Herst, who put together the directory. "And so far as I know, we've never had a problem of abuse. A great deal of cooperative spirit has been built up over the years, and this is one way we help each other. If you break somebody's slide projector, naturally you fix it before returning it."

Other available services include the use of addressograph, ditto, mimeograph, Gestefax and Gestefont, offset, spirit duplicator, and Xerox machines. Herst, who is administrator of the K. A. M. Isaiah Israel Congregation, happens to have one of the larger photocopiers in the association, and her modest per-copy charge "pays for more than half the rental of the machine," she says. "If the other churches and synagogues weren't using it, we probably couldn't afford a copier of this size."

The second part of the directory lists suppliers recommended by the council members — from altar candle sources to florists to piano tuners to window washers. "By listing these people, we don't necessarily endorse them," Herst explains. "We're simply saying that someone in our association has had a good experience doing business with them. Members are welcome to call me for the name of the recommending church or synagogue in order to find out more if they like."

FINANCES

Salaries: a Calm Approach

Few issues seem touchier than setting pastoral salaries. Boards often flounder trying to negotiate pay scales and raises amiably.

Life Center Church in Reno, Nevada, has found a way to avoid frustration by letting each staff member know what to expect.

"We took salary negotiations out of the board meetings and created a policy that would be handled administratively," says Pastor David Fritsche. "The policy personalizes the wages paid, but depersonalizes the process of setting the wages."

Life Center uses an annual survey of other churches to determine average salaries for pastors, secretaries, and custodians, but its unique idea is the set of adjustments that follow:

- *Educational qualifications* (ministerial staff only)

High school — average minus 10 percent

Bachelor's degrees from recognized school — average

Master's degree from recognized school — average plus 7.5 percent

Doctor's degree from recognized school — average plus 15 percent.

For each additional degree in a field that would improve ministry skills — an additional 2.5 percent.

- *Experience qualifications outside Life Center*

0-1 years — average minus 2 percent

2-5 years — average

More than 5 years — average plus 2 percent.

- *Experience at Life Center*

0-1 years — average minus 2 percent

2-5 years — average

6-10 years — average plus 3 percent

More than 10 years — average plus 6 percent.

"Now as inflation or deflation occurs, we are better stewards of both our finances and personnel," says Fritsche. "Our six staff members are happy, and so is the board of elders, because they no longer have to wrangle each year over salaries."

A Tax Exemption for the Asking

Pastor Roger Dennis took a second look at his church's utility bill one day and noticed a curious line: "Sales Tax." Weren't churches such as his (Faith Lutheran, Wichita Falls, Texas) and other nonprofit organizations exempt from such payments?

A little investigation revealed the answer: Yes — *if you ask*.

"We had been paying both a city and state tax on electricity and gas," says the pastor. "A simple phone call to the utilities was all it took to stop the tax and also get a rebate." The savings amounted to between 3 and 4 percent of the bill.

Next Dennis called some of his fellow clergy or church administrators and found most of them unaware of the ruling that said exemption had to be requested. One pastor of a larger church said, "I wouldn't have thought to check the utility bills. We simply receive them and pay them."

The same exemption usually applies to church-owned parsonages. While laws vary from state to state, utility taxes are certainly worth researching and eliminating if possible.

A Fun-Raiser

How can you create laughter and suspense, spark creativity, encourage church members to serve one another, and raise money for a worthy cause all at the same time?

Emmanuel Christian Community in Richmond, British Columbia, enjoyed all those elements when they held a "Service Auction." Besides the fun and fellowship for the 40 members who participated, over $2,000 was raised for World Vision.

Several weeks before the event, a sign-up sheet was posted, and people were encouraged to be creative in thinking of services to offer.

"We especially wanted the kinds of service that involved people spending time together," says Eleanor Spruston, who helped plan the event.

By the night of the auction, 50 items were listed and sold:

- A dozen homemade muffins to be delivered each week for a month went to $7.
- A teenager's offer to tune up a 10-speed bike went for $15.
- A window-washing job went for $65. ("We knew the man who eventually bought it had a huge house, so we bid him up," says Spruston with a grin.)
- A five course gourmet dinner for four went for $85 to two couples who pooled their funds.

"We had a wide variety of services offered," says Spruston. "A dentist offered to tidy up a yard. Others offered oven cleaning, baby sitting, an afternoon of sailing, a series of three racquetball or guitar lessons — gifts of time, talent, and love. And when the bidding was done and the money collected, the benefits had barely begun. We still had the services to be enjoyed, skills to be shared, and new friends to be formed."

After their good experience, Spruston offers the following secrets:

1. While it's not necessary to have a professional auctioneer, choose someone who will keep bidding brisk and inject a little humor.

2. Collect full payment that evening. Be prepared with change and receipts.

3. Instruct each *volunteer* to take initiative to contact the buyer and arrange a time to render his or her service.

Better Than a Cake Sale

When the members of Reba Place Church in Evanston, Illinois, discovered that a rotting beam was going to cost several thousand dollars to fix, they dug a little deeper for their offerings. But paying off the bill would have taken a good deal longer if Linas Brown, one of the congregation leaders, hadn't thought of working off the debt as a group.

How?

By doing inventory for a local store. Those with little spare money could still give an evening of simple work.

So they canceled a midweek service (time already reserved in people's schedules) and trekked instead to Evanston's Marshall Field and Company, a six-floor department store that does over $8 million worth of business a year.

On a cold January evening, the doorman signed in 78 church people for a half-hour orientation and then about three hours of work alongside many of the store's 171 regular employees.

"We're very glad to have you," welcomed Mariam Federgren of the book department. "Maybe this time we won't be here till 4:30 in the morning."

For the church people, it was a good chance to work together and meet new folks. And by 10:30 P.M., the church's roof debt was $1,200 closer to retirement.

Six months later Joyce Gelick, assistant personnel manager and store trainer, called again to request help. "I've talked to all eight department managers, and they felt you did such an excellent job last time that we'd like to have you back for another inventory," she said. "What we appreciated most was the team effort and good spirit you brought."

It was also to her advantage, of course, to have everyone from the same place so she didn't need to worry about honesty and security.

The church budget was no longer in the red, but a new ministry to 80 Cambodian refugees had been started. Extra funds were needed. So on a humid summer evening, 73 church adults again went from their regular jobs or homes down to the store to put in a few more hours of counting socks and shirts and candles . . . and serving the Lord together.

Reported by Dave Jackson

A Parable Revisited

When Quentin Larson preached on the parable of the talents, he closed with a daring call for application. He spread $500 of borrowed money — tens, fives, and ones — across the front of Grace Covenant Church, Stambaugh, Michigan, and invited his audience to come take what they wanted.

Their task: to imitate the two faithful servants in Matthew 25 and multiply the money in order to finance a summer camping ministry.

Would the dollars evaporate? Would any increase be realized?

At an all-church potluck a month later, the totals were announced. The original $500 was recouped, plus the 8 percent interest due — plus $1,900 for the camping program!

Members excitedly told how they used their talents:
- Some sewed baby clothes and quilts and sold them.

- One baked 75 pounds of rye bread and sold each pound loaf for $1.50.
- Another baked coffee cakes and sold them for $80 in order to buy supplies for an Italian dinner. Thirty guests then bought tickets to enjoy the feast.
- Others served spaghetti dinners.
- The High League (high school group) served a pancake breakfast with their original funds and donated the increase.
- On cleaning day at nearby Covenant Point Bible Camp, several children sold Kool-Aid.
- Others made hair barrettes and sold them for $1.50 each.

An entire congregation was thus motivated not only to finance an outreach but also to experience a key spiritual truth in the process.
Reported by Audrey Carli

Tithing with Satisfaction Guaranteed

The thought of giving away 10 percent of your income can be scary, especially if you've never done it regularly.

That's why John Clark offered a money-back guarantee to those at Trinity Assembly of God in Comstock, Michigan, who were willing to try tithing. "Last April I introduced a 90-day 'Prove Me Challenge" to the people, based on Malachi 3:8-12," says Pastor Clark. "Many in the church were having financial difficulties and didn't feel they could tithe faithfully. What they needed was some sort of encouragement to step out in faith."

The challenge: to give at least 10 percent of their income plus at least $1 per week in offerings for the next 90 days. If God did not meet their needs during that time, the church would refund the full recorded amount given.

What happened?

● Many who had never tithed before signed a commitment card. "If the church believes in it that much, it must work," said one member.

"It did work," says Clark. "No one has asked for a refund."

● Giving increased. Offerings the previous three months had averaged $737 a week; during the challenge (May-July), they averaged $864. "And that's even more encouraging since offerings usually drop off as summer begins," the pastor says.

"The results of the challenge have been so good that we're extending it indefinitely."

WHY WE STOPPED PASSING THE OFFERING PLATE

by Dennis Sawyer, pastor, Philadelphia Church, Chicago

"You forgot to take the morning offering again, Pastor," said head usher Dick Ford in a rather bewildered tone. (He was also a deacon and a trustee.) It was true. Nearly a year into my first pastorate, I was still, on occasion, forgetting to pause for the collection of tithes and offerings.

Now and then I was spared embarrassment when an anxious usher would frantically wave his money from behind the last pew or hand me a note just before I started the morning message. The problem was mine. I had grown up hearing non-Christians say, "All the church wants is your money." When I opened my mailbox or turned on a Christian broadcast, I had to agree that money seemed paramount in the kingdom of God.

Besides, the offering just didn't seem to fit anywhere. We were seeing a spiritual awakening in that small coastal Oregon town of 500. The Sunday morning attendance had grown from 200 to 300 during the year, with a special sense of God's presence in each service. To pause and take an offering seemed tangential. We tried taking it at the beginning of the service, and people thought we seemed too anxious to get their money. In the middle of the service, it interrupted the flow, and at the end it interfered with the altar call or concluding challenge of the message.

At the peak of frustration, while preparing a sermon on tithing from Malachi 3:10, I was pierced by the words "Prove me now, saith the Lord of Hosts." A series of questions deluged my mind:

Could God provide for our financial needs without our passing the plate?

Does the worship of giving have to occur at a fixed moment betwen 11:00 and 12:15 Sunday mornings?

If we freed ourselves from passing the plate, could we better use that time in another form of corporate worship?

What does Scripture mean when it says not to let your left hand know what your right hand is doing so that your giving may be in secret (Matt. 6:3)?

A few days later I presented a challenge to the official church board. "Let's mount offering boxes on the wall at each sanctuary exit and discontinue the collection of tithes and offerings during our services."

After they recovered from shock, the comments began to fly. I remember parts of the exchange:

Question: "Is it scriptural?"

Answer: "Yes. It's what Jehoiada, the priest, did in 2 Kings 12, for example. He took a chest and bored a hole in its lid. He placed it beside the altar, on the right side as people entered the temple, to collect their gifts.

"Mark 12:41 tells about Jesus sitting down across from where the crowd put their money into the temple treasury. That's where he spotted the widow with the two coins.

"Even the apostle Paul mentioned in 1 Corinthians 16:2 that he wanted their money set aside before he came so there wouldn't have to be a collection after he arrived."

Question: "But isn't giving an act of worship? Doesn't it belong in a worship service?"

Answer: "Yes, it's an act of worship. But so is visiting prisoners and feeding the hungry, yet we don't squeeze all of that into the Sunday morning service."

Our discussion ended in a compromise. The church board requested that one box be placed low enough for children (a great idea), that an appropriate notice appear in each Sunday's bulletin so people would know how to contribute, and that the whole concept be reviewed after three months.

In fear and trembling, we mounted the boxes, stopped passing the offering plate, and waited. For six weeks the income ran far below normal. People would bring their tithes to church and take them home again. On the seventh week the "Lord of hosts" began to pour out his blessings. People who normally gave a dollar a week realized they hadn't donated in a long time, so they suddenly wrote out checks for $25 and $30 to make up.

Of greater importance, however, was our accelerated attendance, which soon averaged over 500 and increased to 1,200 on Easter or other special events. People said things like "I never realized how much the boxes on the wall meant to me until I brought a friend to church and we didn't take an offering. He was overwhelmed."

"I like it because it takes away the feelings of obligation; I know I give more with this system."

The offerings continued to be collected via the boxes for our six remaining years in Hammond, Oregon. God "proved" himself again and again.

When I began my pastorate a year and a half ago here in the inner city of Chicago, I immediately requested that we stop passing the collection plate and use that segment of time for personal prayer instead. The leadership agreed to give it a try, and now toward the beginning of each service the elders come forward and make themselves available to pray for the needs of the people. People come for prayer while the rest of the congregation worships in song.

I warned everyone about the six-week dip — with the result that people overcompensated, and it never happened! During the first year of using boxes in Chicago, we collected more in tithes and offerings than in any previous year. Again, the comments were intriguing:

"When you tithe once a month by check, it was always a bit disconcerting to have an offering plate put under your nose for the next three weeks."

"I think it's great, because it avoids all the panic of rummaging through your purse trying to write a check before the usher gets to your pew."

"It's funny, but my favorite time on Sundays has become those moments after the service. I just stay in my seat for a while reflecting on the service and what has been said; then I pray, write a check as the Lord leads, and drop it in the box on my way out. It's a good feeling."

My wife encountered a real "cheerful giver" one morning. The woman was madly stuffing the box with everything she could find in her purse. When my wife said hello, she replied, "I've never been here before, but this is the greatest idea I've ever seen, and I'm voting to keep it that way" — as she kept thrusting her green "votes" into the box.

"Each man should give what he has decided in his heart to give, not reluctantly or under compulsion, for God loves a cheerful giver" (2 Cor. 9:7, NIV).

Paying Less for the Same Items

Does a local church qualify for wholesale prices on its many purchases?

Absolutely, says Carl G. Conner, pastor of First Assembly of God in Toledo, who's turned wholesale purchasing into an art form throughout his years in the ministry. "A church is a corporation, not an individual, and almost every item it buys in quantity can be gotten wholesale," he claims, ticking off such lists as:

- *Paper products:* copy paper, hand towels, toilet tissue, cups, plates . . .
- *Janitorial supplies:* soap, cleaners, wax, deodorizers . . .
- *Foodstuffs,* especially if the church operates a school or day care program.
- *Office supplies:* pencils, staples, paper clips . . .

With a little comparison shopping, Conner quickly cut his cost of photocopier paper from $3.50 a ream (at a retail supply firm) to $2.63 a ream in lots of 50 reams.

"Not every firm with the word *wholesale* in its name gives wholesale prices," Conner warns. "One company was charging us $1.47 for a can of industrial cleaner. I called the supplier and said, 'Bob, our costs are too high. We can't afford you anymore.'

"Right away he admitted that we hadn't really been buying wholesale. The price of a *large* can of cleaner soon came down to $1.14.

"So I asked for a new price list. Page 1 of the new list contained 12 items. If we'd purchased one of each (mostly cases) under the old prices, we would have spent $496.68. The new total turned out to be $425.06 — a 14½ percent drop. All I had to do was ask."

Many *retailers* can give a church wholesale prices, Conner has learned. But if they won't, head for the Yellow Pages.

Cheaper by the Skid

Two dozen churches and other ministries in Athens, Ohio, may not agree on all the fine points of doctrine, but they have certainly gotten their heads together on purchasing office supplies. A secretaries' cooperative is buying paper for one-third of retail and saving money on a wide selection of mimeographing supplies as well.

"We pool our orders every September, December, and March," explains Jeanne Donado of United Campus Ministry, one of the co-op's three coordinators.

"Last time, for example, we bought around 700 reams of paper, several cartons of mimeo stencils, and several cases of ink."

The other two coordinators are Sharon Perry of First United Methodist Church and Angela Carbetta of Christ Lutheran Church, where the supplies are delivered each time. Members must pick up their orders within two working days.

The co-op continues to grow rapidly as more churches learn about the savings of bulk buying. "Last year, " says Donado, "I saved our office almost $500."

THE 0% SOLUTION

by Jerry Bryan, pastor, Beracah Bible Church, Amarillo, Texas

The only time a church mortgage gives any cause to celebrate is when it's burned. Otherwise, it's a drain on resources. Interest payments can easily triple or quadruple the cost of a church building.

Beracah Bible Church decided to forgo the joy of mortgage burning for something better: no mortgage at all.

When we began back in 1963, our board of trustees quickly agreed that the congregation would function on a "pay-as-you-go" basis. Simply put, this policy allows us to spend only the money already in hand. Two factors led to this decision:

• Several churches and religious organizations in our area had been financially irresponsible, thus tainting the reputation of the rest of us. They assumed huge debts for building projects as a "step of faith." In reality, it was a step of presumption. They were convinced it was "God's will," but it became a stone of burden for the whole Christian community.

Their desperate appeals for funds and their defaulting on payments created a negative image. Banks were reluctant to foreclose on religious organizations, but they weren't eager to deal with any new churches, either.

• We had no significant borrowing power anyway. Our only collateral would have been the personal property of members, which is what banks were demanding. Rather than asking individuals to cosign, our trustees unanimously endorsed a policy of nonindebtedness. It has served us well for over 19 years.

For the first 15 years, we were content to meet in a series of nine locations for nominal rent, sometimes only the cost of utilities. We started with five families who gathered for worship in a vacant bank building. Later we used the hospitality room of another bank and eventually moved into a house, where we grew to 125.

At first the makeshift locations didn't bother people; they came for content, not surroundings. But soon the surroundings were interfering with the ministry. We literally had people sitting on one another's laps.

"I'm not coming on Sunday morning anymore," one lady told me. "There's no place to sit. I'll come to weeknight things, but Sunday is just too crowded."

After three more moves, our people were ready to forsake the nomadic life. The final straw came when we discovered we could be locked out; one Sunday, for instance, "our" meeting place was preempted by an antique show.

It was then, in 1977, that our policy against deficit spending got its greatest test. Already the cash policy had been successful in paying for several church automobiles, a van, and a parsonage. But the estimated $200,000 for a modest auditorium and land to expand was a much larger challenge.

One secret to successfully raising money before the construction, we discovered, was to take immediate action. People will give "green money" — their liquid assets, such as checking account funds, while a project is still in the talking stage. But our farmers usually don't spend their "brown money" — funds invested in the soil — until they see the project actually begin. People don't like to donate larger sums and then have the church just sit on them. They'd rather have it earning interest until it's needed.

So we did three things:

1. We promised donors that their gifts would be invested in a high-interest-bearing fund until the bills started coming in. Thus, we asked them to donate both principal and the potential interest to us, but we, in turn, would be good stew-

ards and invest it wisely until it was needed.

2. We promised that the money would be used only for the building project. If plans for the construction fell through, we would return their money to them *with the interest earned.*

3. We began the construction as soon as we could. Our designer and builder, Marvin Winton, a professional home builder and member of our board of trustees, estimated the amount necessary to erect only the enclosed shell of the building. We didn't want a half-finished building deteriorating in the weather.

When that amount was received, we held a groundbreaking ceremony, and construction began on our 400-seat auditorium. Our hope was that, once begun, the building project would not have to be interrupted by lack of funds.

As the foundation was being dug, we were still $34,000 short of what we needed to complete the interior of the building. Humanly speaking, our resources were drained. Our 150 people had given cheerfully and sacrificially. It seemed unreasonable to assume that they could make up the deficit in time. But before the concrete was poured for the foundation, the rest of the money was in hand.

On the day the cement trucks arrived the pour the foundation, my wife went to the mail chute and opened an envelope addressed to the church. The return address was a bank in Midland, Texas, some 250 miles south of Amarillo. Incredulously, she stared at a cashier's check for $37,000. This was, of course, $3,000 more than we actually needed to complete the building; that money was later used to landscape the grounds and give the place a truly finished look.

Where did the money come from? We still don't know. We knew that Midland Bible Church, our sister church, has a faithful ladies' prayer band, which incessantly prayed for our building needs. The precise connection between that prayer group and the anonymous gift remains a mystery to us all.

On Easter Sunday, 1978, we opened the doors for the first worship service in our new debt-free building amid great rejoicing.

This financial policy cannot be explained in terms of a series of lucky breaks; 19 years is too long for a policy to work by luck. No, we don't believe our approach is the only scriptural position, but God has honored our conviction.

Since that time, we have built a much-needed expansion to our building, including a larger nursery and more Sunday school classrooms. Our policy was the same: We would continue construction only as long as the funds held out. As the paint was drying on the new walls, the last of the $180,000 cost was freely given.

Our congregation has grown steadily in a city that is not growing; our Sunday morning attendance is now 275. We have never been underwritten by people of great means. Most of our donations have been in the $100 range, and almost all of them sacrificial.

Our faith has been strengthened. We feel we've learned not to presume upon God, but to wait upon him. As Hudson Taylor put it, "God's work done in God's way will never lack God's supply."

Strangers at the Door

A shabbily dressed stranger walks into the church office wanting money for a meal.

A needy mother explains she can't come up with the rent money this month.

A transient needs a place to spend the night and asks to sleep in the church. What do you do?

The Church of the Nazarene in Newberg, Oregon, is located near a highway and averages three or four outsiders a month asking for help.

"With the present economy, I've noticed an increase in the number of people who really need help," says Pastor Bill O'Connor. "These aren't the "professional transients," but people recently unemployed who are on their way to Portland looking for work. Sometimes they run out of money and need bus fare to make it the rest of the way.

"Since I'm the one most often called upon to deal with these people, our church board set up a special Pastor's Discretionary Fund to help."

That fund — an interest-bearing checking account — has a $250 monthly limit. Whenever a worthy need comes along, O'Connor writes a check. Anything spent is replaced at the first of each month, when O'Connor submits to the board his written report of the fund's activity.

"We don't give funds directly to the person asking," he says. "We have a credit arrangement with a nearby restaurant and motel. Sometimes we'll make out a check to the grocery store, landlord, or bus company. That way we make sure the money is used as intended.

"The fund works well and eliminates the need of turning deserving persons away for lack of resources."

A Cure for Double-Dipping

Churches in the small prairie towns along Interstate 70 east of Denver get a steady flow of travelers asking for money. "We're only three blocks off the highway," says Paul L. King of Deer Trail Friends Community Church, "and the people who come to our church door often try the other churches as well, just going down the line."

To prevent multiple handouts and also to spread the financial load, King and half a dozen other pastors in the four-town ministerial alliance set up a cooperative fund with a voucher system. "Each participating church puts $50 a year into the fund, and more as needed," he explains. "We also raise money through offerings at the Good Friday and Thanksgiving community services."

In order to disburse funds, a church first phones the association treasurer for authorization, giving information about the traveler in need — name, address, car model, color, and license number. Anyone trying to collect twice is thus quickly exposed.

Qualified persons are then given a voucher for $5 to $10 worth of gas or food at a specified service station, grocery store, restaurant, or motel — all of which have agreed to bill the association. No cash is handed out. The voucher includes not only information about the traveler but also the signature of the authorizing pastor and the date (including year, to prevent reuse or duplication).

"We ask to see a driver's license or ID," King adds, "in order to spot anyone involved in illegal activities. We also usually ask for work in return — mowing grass at the church, weeding, painting, or cleanup. And people do it — if they're truly in need."

"Hey, Pastor, Can You Spare a Buck?"

Not all tourists who come to Cape Cod bring enough money. That makes things awkward for pastors such as John Michael at First Baptist Church in West Harwich, when strangers drop in seeking aid.

In addition to providing a meal at a restaurant a block away (billed directly to the church, so no cash has to be handed out), Michael frequently offers the chance to do some work around the church for wages. Many supplicants decide they're not that desperate, but some are willing.

"I was getting disgusted at not being able to appraise these people and their stories," the pastor remembers. "Local needs are one thing, where we can do some investigating, but often it's young people who are stranded, looking for a job, maybe on drugs — who knows? We couldn't just keep passing out funds.

"So six years ago the deacons set up a new policy. It takes the decision off my shoulders and puts it on the person who's asking — and it's been a great relief." A young man in his 20s, for example, spent two days last fall scraping and painting, trimming hedges, and cutting the lawn, for which he was paid $3.50 an hour. A man in his middle 40s put in five hours raking leaves in order to earn cash.

"I keep a list of things that need to be done," says Michael, "checking with the custodian periodically, especially for jobs that require climbing. The young drop-ins can be a real help to us with that. Meanwhile, they save their pride."

A Fair Way to Share

When the steel mills closed in Youngstown, Ohio, in 1980, the economic problems had only begun. The ripple effects of the recession pushed area unemployment over 20 percent by 1982.

Tabernacle Evangelical Presbyterian Church wasn't exempt; 12 percent of its household heads were out of work.

"We wondered how to help our people who'd lost their jobs," says Pastor Robert Ralston. "Traditionally, any dire financial needs are met by a Deacon's Fund, but that requires people to apply, to come asking for financial help. This situation seemed to call for something else."

Their solution? A special offering on the last Sunday morning of each month was divided equally among all the families where the head of house was unemployed.

"This eliminated the indignity of applying to the Deacon's Fund and any possible ill will about the amount any one individual might receive," says Ralston.

"The beauty of the idea was its simplicity and effectiveness. If you were out of work, a member of the church, and the head of a household, you were going to receive a check within a week of the offering."

Month after month, offerings of $500 to $800 were given by the 200 attenders to be divided among up to a dozen families.

"Now almost everyone is working again, thank the Lord," says Ralston. "But we're keeping this idea on file for future needs. Many people were blessed to give and blessed to receive."

WHY WE LOAN GOD'S MONEY

by Larry Parker, administrator, Christ Church of Northgate, Seattle

Neither a borrower nor a lender be:
For loan oft loses both itself and friend.
Hamlet, Act I, Scene 3

If there is a poor man among your brothers . . . do not be hard-hearted or tightfisted. Freely lend him whatever he needs.
Deuteronomy 15:7-8

Churches have traditionally sided more with Shakespeare than Moses when it comes to the thorny matter of helping members financially. Many have assumed that loaning church funds to individuals would only cause trouble, trigger gossip, alienate those who fall behind in repayment, and drain the church's resources.

Over the last eight years at Christ Church, an Assembly of God congregation of some 1,700, we have worked toward a goal of financial maturity among our people. We also want them to feel cared for in a practical way. Like many churches, we make outright gifts — benevolences — to members who are unemployed or in other difficulty. At other times, it seems the best approach is to grant the person a small, no-interest loan.

We presently have about $8,000 outstanding in amounts averaging $250. Because we tie our giving and lending to financial instruction and counseling, our defaults have run less than 2 percent (almost all of them in cases where the person was loosely associated with the body).

Consider this statement from a single mother: "When I lost my job recently, my parents saw how the family of believers helped me with food, rent, and utilities — how they cared. That spoke more than 100 sermons or anything I ever shared with them about the Lord. They cried."

Our sharing at Christ Church happens on two different levels.

- *Institutional caring.* We loan money from the common purse, and we also make gifts (about $20,000 last year). Recent federal budget cuts means churches cannot look to welfare and social benefits as much as in the past. I believe this is as it should be. We, the church, must resume this responsibility we abdicated years ago.
- *Home fellowship caring.* Our 40 small groups often take care of smaller needs directly without coming to me for institutional help. One group recently collected money among themselves to buy auto parts for a widow in the group. The men then did the repairs.

Another group has, over a two-year period, paid the tuition for a single mother's two boys to attend our Christian school.

Another family needed major roof repairs. In this case, the two levels collaborated: the church bought the materials, while the brothers in the home group provided the labor to fix the roof.

Needs usually come to my attention through the home group leaders. A single unemployed mother recently shared with Bob Hamack that she was worried about her utility bills. Bob, after making sure the need was legitimate, phoned Dennis Trout, an elder who oversees him and several other home group leaders. The two men then came to me with a recommendation for aid from the common purse.

In this way we build a healthy sense of community, interdependence, and shared life. People feel loved and cared for by a personal God who works through his people. The gospel has a demonstrable influence on the way we live and care.

Prudent Guidelines

1. At Christ Church, we do not feel responsible to meet the needs of all the poor in Seattle or even our immediate neighborhood. Our directive in Deuteronomy 15 has to do with "brothers." This does not preclude reaching further as the Lord directs, but it does give a boundary to our ongoing responsibility.

So we seldom grant loans or benevolences to new people in the fellowship. Our other caring ministries — the food bank, children's clothing co-op, job-finding workshops, job-matching service, and counseling — are open to them, of course. But with rare exceptions, things have not gone well when we've made a financial investment in a new member.

2. We set dollar limits. I am authorized to loan up to $500 on my own judgment; above that, I consult with a designated elder, and we decide together. For loans of more than $1,000, I go to the elders as a group.

In the area of benevolences:

- A gift of $25 can be made by any one of the pastors, elders, or home group leaders.
- A gift of $26-100 requires two signatures.
- A gift of more than $100 requires three signatures (the home group leader, the overseeing elder, and myself), plus an effort to determine if financial counseling is advised.

3. Borrowers are asked to sign a dotted line. They receive repayment coupons just like at any bank. But the letter of agreement they sign puts the loan in a special light:

You shall not be bound by this note as the world would bind you. We are a family here, the family of God. We would encourage you to be a faithful steward of that which God has entrusted you to care for. Should you, during the term of this agreement, fall short of your own expectations and the terms upon which we have agreed, please contact us that we might communicate honestly and openly. . . . This agreement shall bear no interest except the debt of love which binds us together.

How to Get Started

Churches that believe God's favor and blessing rest upon those who attend to the poor can begin with these steps.

● *First, entreat the Lord for vision.* You must be convinced that the Scripture calls you to this ministry of caring, or it will become mechanical and heartless — another welfare system. The congregation must share the vision as well as the leadership.

● *Establish clear boundaries and authority limits for those making decisions,* as illustrated above.

● *Choose persons of integrity who have demonstrated a godly standard in the areas of money and possessions.* Those who administer the funds and counsel with the needy must exemplify maturity and also wisdom.

● *Go ahead; take some risks.* As soon as you begin actually giving and loaning, you will learn to identify the difference between *"needs"* (Deut. 15:8) and materialistic thirst or lack of discipline. You will eventually be taken advantage of, and sometimes you will not even receive a thank-you. But it will be counted to you as righteousness.

● *Be strong enough to say no sometimes.* After guiding a person through an analysis of where he stands financially, you may realize that the wise thing to do is to challenge him to work it out alone. Remember that your goal is more than to relieve financial pain; it is to help the person toward maturity.

● *Bolster your giving/lending with financial seminars, teaching, and counseling.* Help people understand the principles of godly stewardship. In earlier years I did a large amount of financial counseling, but now I am down to roughly three hours a week as our people have matured in this area. The home group leaders are able to give on-the-spot direction in many situations, so that I see only the more difficult cases.

● *Keep communication lines open with borrowers.* If they are unable to keep up with their obligations, they may succumb to a burden of guilt that alienates them from God and the fellowship. Let them know your love goes on regardless.

The strength of such a ministry lies not in the dollars themselves but in relationship. On the surface, the church may be helping someone buy a wood stove or enabling a young couple needing an apartment to come up with their first and last months' rent. But at a deeper level, the undershepherds of Christ are tending his flock. This is a ministry of caring enough to know the real needs, and knowing enough to care.

SCHEDULING

A Different Rhythm
for Sunday Morning

How many North Americans think church services
run too long?

Only a pollster could tell for sure, but the people
who started Community Bible Fellowship in Azusa,
California, a few years ago decided to address the
objection anyway. They split their morning worship into
two halves, with coffee and doughnuts between.

"We begin at 9:30 with a few choruses, a prayer,
and then the sermon right away — when people are
awake and attentive!" says David DeLoach, associate
pastor. "Our children are in Sunday school during that
time. At about 10:20 we introduce visitors, make
announcements, and then take a half-hour break."

Community Bible Fellowship is a daughter of Sierra
Madre Congregational Church and currently involves
about 90 people. It meets in a school and has access to
kitchen facilities. "The fellowship time kind of energizes
everyone again for the second half, which begins at
10:55," DeLoach continues. "The children join us then
for singing, prayer, sharing, and on some Sundays,
Communion. By 11:30, we're finished."

The break, of course, lets some people show up late
or leave early, but this has not proven to be a major
problem so far. "We've attracted a number of people
who were not comfortable in a more structured church.
People like the informality of our schedule."

Moving "Sunday Night" to Sunday Morning

When the Church of Christ in Dixon, Illinois, decided to discontinue its traditional Sunday evening service, it didn't just leave a vacuum.

Instead, it organized Sunday morning into three one-hour sessions: Bible classes, then the regular worship assembly, and finally a special time that varies each week.

"We didn't want to forfeit that extra hour together," explains Tom Wadsworth, the minister, "and we wanted to accomplish a number of biblical directives that were somehow falling by the wayside. So we set up a rotation."

First Sunday of the month: Exhortation Sunday. Different men of the church give planned or spontaneous exhortations and encouragements.

Second: Singing Sunday. Everyone sits by section (soprano, alto, tenor, bass) for an hour of favorite songs.

Third: Burden-bearing Sunday. The church breaks into small groups to share, using questions like "What tests your faith?" or "When is being a Christian easiest/hardest?"

Fourth: Feedback Sunday. Members talk back to the minister about his sermon that day, which has been planned to stimulate discussion.

Fifth (four times a year): Super Sunday Celebration, a potluck to honor new Christians.

"Each week we serve coffee and refreshments between the second and third sessions," Wadsworth adds. "It's an excellent way to meet visitors and entice them to stay for the last session. We get almost 100 percent retention from the second hour, and people are growing and getting to know one another better. The ever-changing schedule keeps excitement and variety in every Sunday."

Where Sunday Night Thrives

Summertime means peak attendance at the Sunday evening service of Raccoon Presbyterian Church, Aliquippa, Pennsylvania. The normal figure of 40 to 50 more than doubles during July and August.

That's because they take the service outside.

An inexpensive pavilion has been built on a farm, complete with piano and chairs brought from the church, only eight minutes away. Corn grows in the field 20 feet to the left. Signs along the road and posters in town store windows direct visitors though the western Pennsylvania hills to the site.

"Our evening together has two parts," Pastor Robert W. Bradbury explains. "The 7:00 service includes a good deal of music — from our choir, from my own five children, who all play instruments, and from visiting groups. We line up pastors from the area to speak along a common theme throughout the summer, and they often bring musical talent as well as other parishioners with them."

Following the service, a campfire is lit, and 80 to 90 percent of the crowd lingers to talk, roast wieners, share cups of coffee, and sing some more in the twilight. "It's a good fellowship time for young adults," says the pastor, "and for all of us."

One summer schedule even included a minicrusade in late July with a guest musical group: afternoon concert, covered-dish supper, then the evening service.

"Not only is an outdoor service less threatening to some who might not come to a church building," Bradbury says, "but with the backdrop of farmland and God's beautiful scenery, it is also a fitting location for worship at the close of the Lord's day."

Community Christian Church in the small town of Barnes City, Iowa, preserves its indoor 6:00 service — but shortens it the last Sunday of each month to head for the park a block away. There a potluck meal is enjoyed together, followed by volleyball and horseshoes.

"We start as soon as the weather clears," says Pastor Douglas Smiley, "which is often the last Sunday of April. And we can usually run through October."

"We've placed a great emphasis in our church on being a family together, and this is one of the family things we do. The youth and adults all play volleyball together, with a couple of older folk refereeing. Fellowship has really blossomed through these evenings."

Once a summer — usually in July — the entire town and surrounding area is invited to join the congregation for Sunday night in the park. "I believe that at some points, the church needs to be visible in the world — not always closed up inside a building," says Smiley. "So we advertise heavily and draw many from the community who aren't a part of our church. We want them to feel what our family is like."

The overall restructuring of Sunday night — services that give time for informal worship, sharing, and small-group interaction, plus the once-a-month events in the park — has tripled evening attendance.

The T.G.I.F. Service

On Friday evenings, when most workers are fleeing downtown Houston to start their weekends, up to 100 people head for nearby South Main Baptist Church to eat, worship, and study the Bible. This is "Sunday church" for people who must work Sundays and also for those who don't feel comfortable in the more formal traditions of Sunday morning.

"We start at 5:30 with a two-dollar meal in the fellowship hall," explains Linda Jones, minister to adults. "People get to know each other week after week — some of our closest relationships are among this group.

"Then at 7:00 comes the worship service, in the same hall. Dr. Chafin, our senior pastor, preaches the same message he'll deliver twice on the upcoming Sunday, when 1,500 people will hear him in the sanctuary.

"We don't have a Friday night choir, but our minister of music does arrange for special music — solos or small groups. The atmosphere is very informal, laid back; this is the end of the work week, and people kind of unwind together."

Adult Bible study follows for an hour at 8:00, with a choice of four electives. A sharing group for recently released prisoners and families of prisoners meets at the same time.

"When we first started in September, 1979," says Jones, "some people were afraid this would steal people from the Sunday services. If anything, it's been the other way around; some who started coming on Friday nights have gradually become integrated into the Sunday program."

The church offered children's classes at first but discarded them when not enough parents with young children participated. Now, only child care for preschoolers is provided.

"Being a downtown church," Jones adds, "we think there are more people who work downtown who would come if they knew about it. So we've begun some selective newspaper advertising to try to spread the news."

Saturday Night Worship

From Memorial Day to Labor Day each year, the Osakis Lutheran Church of Osakis, Minnesota, holds an extra service — on Saturday night. "We do this for three reasons," says Pastor David Halaas:

1. "Our local farmers like it because then they don't have to rush their farm chores Sunday morning.

2. "We have a resort lake nearby, and the Saturday night service is a point of contact with vacationers from Minneapolis and Fargo.

3. "We have members who work on Sunday mornings at the resort facilities."

The services run from 8 P.M. to 9 P.M. Halaas feels no added strain, but confesses that he *does* have to complete his sermon before Saturday.

The choir takes the summer off, but special music is still included. "Worshiping at night has given us the opportunity to sing some of our evening songs, too," Halaas adds. "Traditionally, Lutherans don't hold evening services, and songs like 'Now the Day Is Over' usually go unsung."

The church advertises its Saturday night worship services in the local newspaper and leaves posters in obvious places around town.

Halaas estimates the evening attendance as 75-140. "I believe at least two thirds (50-100) of these folks would not make it to the Sunday morning service."

But perhaps the greatest benefit goes to the church members themselves. Toward the end of last summer, Alice, a 65-year-old waitress who works summer Sunday mornings in a resort restaurant, told Halaas, "I sure hope you keep the Saturday night services going. It's absolutely the only time I can attend."

If You Can't Stand the Heat . . .

In northern states like Minnesota, churches sometimes hesitate to air-condition their buildings — but on hot summer Sundays, they wish they had. Memories of the long winter don't help much in July when both the temperature and the humidity are in the 90s.

Grace Baptist Church in Austin, Minnesota, came up with an inexpensive solution a few years ago by flip-flopping its morning schedule. The traditional 9:30 Sunday school and 10:45 service are traded at the end of May for:

- 9:00 worship, while the sanctuary is still cool.
- 10:15 Sunday school — a retreat to the downstairs classrooms.

"By the time the day starts to get hot," reports Julie Hansen, a member, "services have ended and people are on their way home to enjoy a long afternoon. Best of all, it doesn't cost a thing!"

Beating Old Man Winter

Weekend blizzards seemed more the rule than the exception during January, 1982, in the upper Midwest. As a result, Sunday worship was hurt badly in many places; members couldn't get to church, and heating bills soared while offerings plunged.

"After we had to cancel two Sundays in a row," says Dale Cope, pastor of Trade Lake Baptist Church six miles west of Frederic, Wisconsin, "the church board met to discuss alternatives. We decided that next time, we wouldn't cancel — we would simply reschedule the service for Monday or Tuesday evening, whenever the storm had eased up a bit."

As it turned out, the winter of '82 didn't force the Trade Lake church to activate its plan, "but we're ready," says Cope. "Our network of caring groups will spread the word by telephone, plus we'll get it announced on the local radio station. We probably won't try to operate Sunday school in the evening, but we'll have a full worship service. Then we'll follow with a potluck, so we can sit around and sympathize with each other about the weather!"

COMMUNICATION

Getting to Know a Congregation

How long does it usually take a new pastor to attach names to faces in a congregation of 250 or more worshipers? How much does it mean to a person to be called by name?

When Dennis Sawyer moved into his new charge at Philadelphia Church in Chicago's inner city, he decided to get on a first-name basis as soon as possible. On the first three Sundays, he asked worshipers to take a few moments to sit for a candid photo in the church foyer.

The result — a pastor's album that not only identifies individuals but also places people into family groupings.

"It was not until I saw the album that I was able to place various young people with their families," Sawyer remarks. The project gave him identifications and insights into the congregation that otherwise would have taken many months.

Reported by Henry Jauhiainen

Paul Sandin made use of First Baptist Church's existing Sector Groups to get better acquainted when he came to the Iowa City church back in 1974. "During September and October of that year," he says, "we invited each of the groups into our home for an evening of fellowship and discussion on our future together." This added up to 12 evenings with an aggregate of about 125 members and friends — roughly a dozen a night.

The evenings had a definite 2½-hour structure:

- 7:30-7:50 Get-acquainted time in small groups of three or four, using questions like "Where were you

born?" "Where did you live when you were five?"
"When and with whom was your first date?"

- 7:50-8:10 Continued small-group reflection on
"What was it that made you choose First Baptist as your
church home?" Sandin then collected the responses
onto newsprint in front of the entire group and asked,
"If these are the reasons you came, what does this say
about our future?"

- 8:10-8:50 Each small group merged with
another, forming groups of six to eight, to discuss,
"What are our greatest assets as a congregation?"
Answers were listed and ranked, then contributed to
another master list on the newsprint pad. "This gener-
ated a lot of comment," says Sandin.

- 8:50-9:10 Refreshment break, served by the
Sandins and the Sector Group leaders.

- 9:10-10:00 Large-group discussion of "What are
your dreams for our church?" The pastor concluded by
challenging the members to view the future as open;
then the evening ended with a prayer circle.

"This was an excellent oportunity for me to learn to
know the people as individuals," Sandin reports. "It also
helped some of the members to meet and talk with
others whom they either did not know or had met only
in worship."

When Sandin moved to his current pastorate in
East Williston, New York, he used the same plan. "The
results were even better. Three or four new programs
came directly from those discussions."

A Double-Duty Answering Machine

Some people hate telephone answering devices, but
not the members of Big Hill Avenue Christian Church in
Richmond, Kentucky.

That's because the machine at their church office not only takes their messages but also gives them valuable information.

"We have two phone lines coming into our building," says Henry D. Mann, Jr., the senior minister. "632-1592 is our regular service; the other is our CARE-RING number, 623-6000. We fill the 30-second recording with late news or events of that particular day before inviting the caller to leave a message.

"We can update a schedule, announce a cancellation, let parents know what time their teens will arrive from camp, set a departure time for some special outing — just about anything. Our folks dial the number regularly to stay informed; it's a great tool."

The CARE-RING number is listed prominently in the phone directory and advertised in church publicity. Whenever bad weather or unusual circumstances force a change of plans, the word is spread within a matter of hours.

A church member dies, and two elders do not hear about it.

A heart patient is rushed to the hospital, and half the church is unaware.

A special board meeting is called, but three board members aren't notified.

Fourth Avenue Church of Christ, Franklin, Tennessee, doesn't worry about these communication problems anymore. A new tape is recorded daily, and members are urged to dial a special phone number to listen to it. The tape runs a minute and a half and contains news of hospital patients, deaths, births, weddings, sermon topics, special meetings and functions, and events taking place in other local churches.

The three staff members take turns recording the day's news, and when they forget, members start calling in asking why. "Many have become pretty dependent on this news line," says Paul Brown, minister of music and education.

Brown doesn't know how many people phone in each day, but many times he's gone to change the tape and the line has been busy.

Members are constantly encouraged to phone in news to the church secretary so it can be transferred to the tape. Usually the tape is recorded each morning, but it's updated regularly when important news bits come in.

If, for some reason, the day is short on news, one of the pastors will record a short devotional. Brown says a lady once told him, "I phoned the news line five times because your devotional message was so good."

The recording unit cost about $100. "It doesn't take messages over the phone; it just gives the ones we've recorded," says Brown.

Nametags for Everyone?

Nametags are sometimes viewed like disarmament: it's a good idea for the other fellow. We enjoy being able to identify others even if we haven't bothered to put a badge on ourselves.

The 227 members of Christ Lutheran Church in Hot Springs Village, Arkansas, have made the decision to wear nametags every Sunday — *everybody*. Upon arrival, each member picks up his tag from a board in the narthex and returns it after the coffee fellowship at the end of the morning. Of the several different designs on the market, this church uses a plasticized version that incorporates a Lutheran Church in America symbol. (Supplier: Western Plastic Products, Box 1429, Long Beach, CA 90801. Price: approximately $1.) A married couple in the church hand-letter the names onto the card stock, which is inserted into the tags. On the back is a spring clip that swivels to any angle for attaching to a lapel or pocket.

Visitors thus do not feel conspicuous when, after signing the guest register, they are asked to fill out a stick-on nametag. Identification has become an accepted part of being present for the day's worship.

"There's no question that it encourages our people to know one another," says Pastor Elmer E. Burrall. "We're in a retirement community, so we get a lot of visitors from up north, and they often comment about how helpful the tags are."

The church began using tags in 1978, a year before Burrall arrived. "It was a great help to me personally in getting to know the parish," he says. "What I appreciate most, however, is being able to use each person's first name during Communion as I serve the cup. I can personalize my words as I present the blood of our Lord to each individual."

That solemn moment almost broke up in laughter one morning, however, when Burrall looked down to see a husband and wife who had inadvertently switched their tags. "Herman was wearing Evelyn's tag and Evelyn was wearing Herman's, and I almost lost my dignity there for a moment. I caught myself just in time to say the right name regardless."

Do some members resist wearing nametags? Not really, says the pastor. "A few people forget to stop by the board, but generally speaking, we have at least 85 percent participation. If someone wears the tag home, he just wears it back to church the next week. So far as I know, we haven't actually had to replace any tags."

Do women object to adding an extraneous tag to a carefully planned outfit? Again, it's not a problem, says Burrall. "Sometimes I'll see the tag clipped to a belt or even a purse if the woman has no lapel or collar that day. But we're all in the habit of using nametags now, and we really appreciate the fact that there's no more fumbling around trying to remember names."

News and Needs

What's happening? Who's ill? Who's out of work? Who has exciting news to share? Church members want to know about each other, not just because they're curious but so they can support and pray for one another.

When worshipers enter the Sunday evening service of Wooddale Church in suburban Minneapolis, an usher hands them a "News and Needs" sheet complied from comments written on registration cards earlier that day.

In the multiple morning worship services, each person is asked not only to register his attendance but also to jot any item of praise, prayer requests to share with the church family, special needs, or announcements. These might include requests for roommates, offers of free car washes, or the arrival of a new grandchild.

The cards are deposited in the offering plates, and a volunteer sorts out the messages and categorizes them. One of the pastoral staff dictates the items quickly onto a tape, doing some on-the-spot editing for consistency and continuity.

A rotating corps of volunteer secretaries comes in several hours before the evening service, transcribes the tape onto mimeo stencils, and runs enough copies for the evening congregation.

"It's been a tremendous aid for 'family communication' in our church body," says senior pastor Leith Anderson. Members also use "News and Needs" throughout the week for prayer reminders in their personal and family devotions. The sheet is occasionally used in guided prayer times in the evening services, and one parishioner reportedly tapes it to the shower wall in order to pray each morning while getting ready for work!

Reported by Terry White

Family-Style Bulletins

Church bulletins usually contain the worship liturgy or order of service, the schedule of weekly events, and maybe a photo of a sunrise over Jerusalem. In at least two churches, however, the bulletins do more.

"The congregation is the family of God, and our bulletins are our family album," says Pastor John Linna of United Lutheran Church, Crystal Falls, Michigan. Photographs of events in the local congregation appear on the back and front covers of the bulletins.

Linna, an amateur photographer, takes the black-and-white pictures with his 35mm camera.

"Since I'm already present at baptisms and weddings, I don't need to set up a a special time for the pictures," he explains. "To get the picture of a senior citizen's birthday party, I may have to make a special trip, but then I have a chance to visit."

Cover photos are a way to introduce new members as well as honor anniversaries, church school classes, and committee workers.

"I happen to enjoy photography, but if a pastor isn't a photographer, an interested layperson could probably be found," says Linna.

The pictures are developed on Thursday, allowing them to be printed by the church's offset press. Before the press was purchased secondhand, the church took the bulletins to an outside printer.

The personalized bulletins are mailed by members to friends and relatives.

"In one case," says Karen Groop, church secretary, "the bulletin of a baptism was sent to a grandmother who had not been able to see the baby yet."

During Lent, only the back cover of the bulletins have photographs. The front covers are made from drawings by fourth, fifth, and sixth graders. Those drawings selected are traced onto a master by the church secretary, so that two or three different ink colors may be used. Chris Bonales, a sixth-grade student, says, "Even though I am still young, it's something I can do to witness for Jesus."

The photo bulletins began in 1977, and the children's drawings in 1978. "All the bulletins are bound at the end of a year, giving the congregation a pictoral as well as a written history," says Pastor Linna.

Reported by Betty Linna

In Clifton, New Jersy, artistic members of Richfield Christian Reformed Church are commissioned to illustrate the bulletin cover with a design based on the day's worship theme.

The artists — sometimes children — are given the Scripture passage ahead of time so they can come up with an original but appropriate black-and-white design. The design is then reproduced on an electronic stencil cutter for the mimeograph machine.

"This way we've begun tapping some talented people who were never given an opportunity to share their gifts in the church before," says Beverly Vander Molen, minister of music and art.

"The first two questions I ask people who are new to the church are 'Do you sing?' and 'Are you an artist?' It works well. I have people lined up to do bulletin covers four months ahead of time.

"People are studying the Word to discover new ideas for themselves. They, in turn, share these ideas through their designs."

Each Sunday the styles and techniques change. "Some people are doing covers who didn't even know they enjoyed drawing," says Vander Molen.

A Good Gossip Column

Bulletins and newsletters can effectively announce events, but it's hard for them to show what a church is *really* like. Lists of meetings and a meditation by the pastor can't capture the personality of a living church.

Janet Bentley and Kathy Dyer, who edit the weekly newsletter at Highlands United Methodist Church in Huntsville, Alabama, found a way to focus on the people of the body.

"We saw people doing things for others, and we'd wish we had a camera," says Bentley. "But since we couldn't get photos, we began to put little verbal pictures in the newsletter."

The feature is called "Glimpses of Highlands . . ." and it's full of items such as:

● *Ed Gullat volunteering some of Highland's little-used equipment to Rev. Jim Berry for use at the new Aldersgate United Methodist Church.*

● *People joyfully gathered in a prayer circle after Gordon Cottrell announced that Pat Palmer had consented to marry him.*

● *Dewey Devaney's face lighting up when sister Peggy came to sit with their family in church.*

● *Amy Freeman making a new friend, Granny Tate, while visiting the elderly at Todd Towers.*

● *Michael Copeland, so little and so well-behaved in church.*

● *Steve Steiner playing "God Gave the Song" as part of his offering to God.*

"We try to illustrate little things you can do that don't cost any money," says Bentley. "We show people giving of themselves."

Kathy Dyer adds, "We want people to know that all the normally unrecognized things are noticed, necessary, and very much appreciated."

According to Pastor Marvin Edmondson, "It helps create enthusiasm and gives incentive to others to get involved."

Keeping Newsletters New

Week-old news isn't news at all. And that's a problem for church newsletters. Sometimes third-class mail delivery can take four days or more, and by the time newletters reach their readers, the "upcoming events" are already over.

Handing them out at church is quick and cheap, but you miss a lot of people that way.

How can you get news out fast, inexpensively, and still ensure that everyone is reached?

First Lutheran Church in Albany, New York, found a solution.

"After years of complaints from members in the suburbs that our monthly newsletter reached them too late," says the church secretary, Jeanette Wiltse, "we came up with the idea of two-part distribution."

On the last Sunday of each month, the bulletin announces, "Pick up your *Crusader* today in the parish house corridor." A table outside the sanctuary contains boxes of already addressed newsletters, presorted by Zip Codes. The most concerned members can get their copies before the first of the month; the rest are taken to the Post Office Monday morning.

"People enjoy glancing at the *Crusader* during our Sunday morning coffee hour," says Wiltse. "And complaints about late delivery have stopped."

When You Wish Upon a Card

Suggestion boxes rarely get much action — they're too much like talking to a tree. Without any response, it's hard to feel you're being taken seriously.

But at Zion Lutheran Church in Montrose, Colorado, suggestions aren't ignored — they're printed in the monthly newsletter.

"When I began my ministry here in October, 1980," says Pastor James Schackel, "the first letter I received came anonymously from a member who wanted me to put out a questionnaire on what people liked and didn't like. It was a symptom of mistrust."

So when it came time to reprint the worship registration card, Schackel added two sections on the back: "I wish . . ." and "I like . . ." with blanks to be filled in. Below is written:

While we are open to anonymous "wishes" and "likes," we hope there is enough trust in this section of the Body of Christ so that will not be necessary. If you feel it is, leave the opposite side of this card blank, and give that information on another card. Reports on "wishes" and "likes" will appear in the ZIONews without names.

"In the two years we've been using this system, it has helped create a very positive feeling among the people," says Schackel.

Last fall, a man wrote that he wished the church would have an old-fashioned mission festival. Schackel brought the item to the church council, and they agreed. An uplifting mission Sunday resulted.

"I don't have too much trouble handling criticisms because there aren't that many," says Schackel. "And when they arise, often the cards themselves take care of it. One person was upset because I showed a film as the sermon one Sunday. The positive cards, however, balanced it out. The person had the opportunity to state her feelings, but she also got to see how others felt."

Three Uses for Video

Among the many ways to utilize video in the church, here are three examples from the Chicago suburbs:

John Manning, youth pastor at Waukegan Bible Church, helped his high school group create a news report on Jeremiah to fit a series of Sunday evening sermons he was preaching. The kids studied Manning's text, brainstormed a script, and began memorizing lines for a program that would include anchormen, news correspondents, "live" interviews, and even commercials.

"We had a lot of fun taping the show," Manning remembers. "We started out with dinner together at the church and then went to work. We kept a monitor on the whole time we were taping. For any mistake, we just rewound the tape and did that segment again. By the time we finished, we'd all learned a lot and gained a great sense of accomplishment."

The video program became the sermon the next Sunday night, with the youth pastor simply adding a brief conclusion.

Many new converts have never seen a water baptism by immersion, says Charles Nestor, former associate pastor at Calvary Temple in Naperville. "And of course, none of them has ever experienced it before — it's truly a once-in-a-lifetime event. So they have a lot of questions and even some fears about the physical mechanics: 'Where do I stand?' and 'Should I cover my mouth and nose?' and 'How long will you hold me under?'"

Nestor relieves such apprehensions by showing the preparation class a short, homemade videotape of immersion. A few minutes of watching answers most of the questions and lets the candidates know exactly what to expect.

In Arlington Heights, "A Day in the Life of Our Savior's Lutheran Church" was created by the stewardship committee last spring for its midyear report to the people. "The purpose was to inform members of the whole range of opportunities their church is providing," says Pastor Richard Jessen. "Few of them had personally seen all the programs and activities we were able to show on the screen."

Highlighting a typical Wednesday, the program included lesser-known things like the church's new counseling center and introduced a newly arrived counselor. Nonparents learned about the 5 to 7 P.M. program for children (grades 3-5) that provides choir training, Bible study, recreation, crafts, and a meal. And along the way, viewers couldn't help noticing that the pastoral day began at 8:00 A.M. and didn't end until 10:30 in the evening.

The videotapes were shown in a series of home meetings organized by neighborhoods. Some members volunteered their playback equipment, while a local video dealer loaned the rest of what was needed. One pastor and a key lay leader were present at each meeting to field questions and collect feedback.

New Members Meet the Past, the Present

One of the helpful tools churches are using to orient new members is a home-produced tape/slide show.

First Church of God in Defiance, Ohio, for example, put together a 12-minute presentation of its various activities, along with a capsule history of the congregation and the special beliefs of its denomination.

The script was written from an outline provided by the pastors, Dick Latham and Dale Senseman, and other lay workers. Various members took the slides, and the final narration was taped by another member who is a local radio broadcaster. The finished product includes an inaudible beep so the slides advance automatically once the tape begins.

"We made several copies of the program so we can show it to small groups in homes," says Latham. "That way we can be sure everyone gets all the information and the same information. The show also helps new members think of questions that might not come up otherwise."

Old First Church (Presbyterian) in Huntington, New York, took time to dramatize its long and colorful history for the camera. Starting with the church's origin back in 1658, when three missionaries arrived to convert the Long Island Indians, the past is retold in full costume. A local redcoat brigade of Revolutionary War buffs portrays the British soldiers who destroyed the church in 1776. The rebuilding in 1784 is highlighted.

As the show moves along, modern scenes present activities a new member might like to join: the choir, the Sunday school, Boy Scouts, Girl Scouts, women's circles, youth groups.

"It's not only educational; it's inspiring and challenging," says William W. Rogers, senior pastor of Old First. "And our committee had a great time creating it to help inform the new ones coming in."
Reported by Betty Steele Everett (Ohio) and William Folprecht (New York)

Bits of Heritage

Most members are at least mildly interested in the history of their congregation — they just won't get around to reading a whole booklet on the subject, no matter how well prepared it is.

First United Presbyterian Church of Paulding, Ohio, came up with a solution a few years ago. For one year, each Sunday's bulletin included "A Second with First Church." These were short reports (3-4 lines) of a specific incident or time from the past.

On the first Sunday of January, the "Second" gave the names of the six men and women who formed the congregation many years before. Other "Seconds" dealt with dates of important events, people, and organizations in the church. Where possible, direct quotes from old records were used. Events were kept in chronological order, and the final weeks reported on present times and some hopes for the future.

By giving church history in small doses, and the same information to everyone at the same time, members were more likely to talk about the past and to feel the tie that binds them to it.

Reported by Betty Steele Everett

The Vacation Map

Every summer, the Christian church in Carmel, Indiana, hangs a big map of the United States to feature all the vacation spots of the church members.

"We wanted our people to feel noticed and missed while they're away for their summer holiday," says Drexel C. Rankin, pastor.

● Each family is encouraged to send the church one postcard while they are gone.

● When received, the cards are placed picture-side-out around the borders of the map.

● Labels bearing the names of each vacationing family are affixed to the cards.

● Finally, a piece of colored yarn is stretched from each family's postcard to its vacation spot.

"We hang the map in an obvious place," says Rankin, "and it usually becomes a gathering place." Between church school and the morning worship service, members will take a cup of coffee, stand around the map, and notice where their fellow parishioners are. Rankin has seen as many as a dozen people clustered at once. "It gives us a feeling that we're together even when we're apart."

The map is about three by five feet, and by the end

of the summer more than 35 families are represented by postcards. The cost, says Rankin, is less than three dollars for the map and yarn. "And if you do it every year," he adds, "your people will really look forward to it."

"You Can't Miss It"?

Lloyd C. Jacobsen, pastor of Bethel Temple in St. Paul, Minnesota, doesn't assume that visitors will automatically know how to find the church. Being located on a secondary street in a metropolitan area, he takes no chances on people getting lost or detoured while on their way to a service.

Each issue of the monthly newsletter includes a standing item: "How to Get to Bethel Temple." In Jacobsen's case, there are two sets of instructions: "From Minneapolis" and "From St. Paul," to accommodate drivers from both directions.

"If someone has decided to try us out," says the pastor, "the last thing we want is for them to have trouble getting to the building. Not everybody is an expert map reader, and lots of lifelong Twin Citians haven't heard of Portland Avenue. So we take care of that problem by giving simple, fail-safe directions. We want to make sure that 'you can't miss it' is a reality, not just a cliché."

The Ghosts
of Christians Past

What about inactives on the membership roll? Should churches clean house occasionally, or is it better to leave the deadwood alone?

Russell F. Blowers, senior minister at East 91st Street Christian Church in Indianapolis, tells a story about two Scottish preachers.

Said the one, "Have you had any additions lately?"

Replied the other, "No, but we've had some excellent subtractions."

Blowers added, "We got courageous and made about 450 'excellent subtractions' five years ago. The process not only tidied up the records but actually reactivated some people who had drifted away. All things considered, it was such a positive experience that we're thinking it's time to do it again."

That's because they didn't just kick people out. A careful sequence of communcation was planned:

• First, a letter went to all inactives explaining the rationale for cleaning the roll — things like "We shouldn't keep your commitment tied up here if you have moved away" and "We shouldn't give an inflated impression of our size to our sister churches and others who ask how many members we have." The point was made that if the recipient was worshiping elsewhere, a transfer really should be arranged.

This letter alone was enough to nudge some people into action.

• A second mailing recapped the first and included a stamped card to return:

☐ I have transferred my church membership to___.

☐ I do not wish to be a member any longer.

☐ I would like to retain my membership.

"We set a deadline of one month," Blowers adds, "and said, 'If we haven't heard from you by then, we will reluctantly proceed to drop your name from the rolls.' "

• The third mailing to nonrespondents announced that they had, in fact, been deleted.

"Sure we got some flak," Blowers admits, "about 'trying to throw people out of the kingdom.' But we got far more good response. 'Thanks for reminding me,' people said or wrote on their cards. Some initiated transfers to the churches where they were active. And a significant number got with it and became active in the church again.

"It was a loving purge that turned out to be healthy for the body as a whole, because it was done prayerfully, forcing people to reexamine their relationships to Christ and his church."

Early Answers to Inevitable Questions

A few miles up the road from the small town of Woodstock, Vermont, lies the Suicide Six Ski Area. Perhaps that had something to do with the village rector's decision back in 1978 to discuss death with his members at St. James Episcopal Church.

Richard Cockrell sent a letter to the church's mailing list of 250 "to enable you to better prepare in heart and mind for such a time when you or a loved one dies." The letter mentioned who to notify when a death occurs (doctor, medical examiner, funeral home, and pastor) and then presented a form to fill out and file with the church. The form, called "Funeral and Burial Plans," covered:

- Names of persons specifying the following details (one person only, or does this apply to several? The entire family?)
- Choice of funeral home
- Burial site
- Other persons beside the pastor to take part in the funeral
- Cremation? If so —
  — Urn or biodegradable container?
  — Memorial service before or after cremation?
  — Ashes to be interred or returned to the family?
- Donation of the body or any organs. If so, to what hospital?

- Site of visiting hours: church? home? mortuary?
- Requests for the service: music, Bible passages or reading, flower arrangements
  - Memorial fund or charity preferences

"We kept a copy in the parish safe," says Cockrell, "returning the original to the individual. We promised confidentiality, of course, and welcomed the person to make changes at any time."

How many members filled out the form? About 20 percent. "Naturally, I didn't hear from the people who didn't want to face their own mortality," says Cockrell, who has since transferred to Williamsville, New York, "but those who did respond were very positive. I sent out the letter again each year and picked up a few more.

"During my tenure, four or five deaths occurred in the church of those who had their plans on file, and it was a great help. Everything was there in writing; the funeral director knew exactly what to do, the family and friends knew, and I knew, without any difficult decisions to be made at such a time."

THE MINISTER'S PERSONAL LIFE

When It's Time to Relax

A mason can go home knowing the bricks are in place.

A reporter can go home knowing the story is written.

But the pastor . . .

When is it time to relax? The job is never done.

James Battey of First Baptist Church in Fairfield, Iowa, wanted to know when he could quit for the day, or the week, and take it easy. So he developed his own Weekly Ministry Report, a form with spaces to write down

- hospital calls
- members visited
- prospects visited
- Bible studies led
- sermons preached
- record of devotional life
- books/articles read
- persons entertained

There are also places to jot notes about recreation, outstanding events, and answers to prayer.

"I fill it out faithfully each week, not to show to any board or committee, but for myself," Battey told an interviewer. "The different sections reflect what I have determined are my priorities, and I have goals for most all of them.

"My goal for calling is 15 per week, and today is Thursday, and I've made 17 already. So I'm relaxing because I know I've done my job."

And the Evening and the Morning Were the Pastor's Day Off

Charles Davis has come up with a novel schedule for his personal day each week: he uses the Jewish system — sunset to sunset. He starts with his day off around 5:00 Monday evening and carries it through to 5:00 Tuesday evening.

Davis, a missionary who works with the Bible Congregation of Caña de Azucar in Maracay, Venezuela, says there are two chief advantages:

• Time with his wife (the evening) falls naturally ahead of time with his three preschoolers (the daytime hours). Each gets a portion of his attention, but the spouse relationship comes first.

• A late evening out doesn't have repercussions for a work day. Tuesday morning can get off to a slow start without problems.

"I also like the fact of having Monday morning and afternoon to plan the week and begin thinking about the coming Sunday," Davis adds. 'It's the right amount of time to get organized — and then take 24 hours off."

Second-Shift Pastoring

Question: How is a church like a pizza parlor?

Answer: Most of the action happens between noon and midnight.

Joe Allison, pastor of Park Forest Church of God in Fort Wayne, Indiana, figured that out when he began analyzing demands on his time. The care of his 100-member flock — visitation, counseling, board meetings, and Bible studies — seemed to be forever crowding out family time.

"I asked myself, 'When is the *best* time for each of these activities?' " The clear answer: evenings, because that's when most lay people are home from work.

So Allison drew up a new schdule:
- *Mornings:* family time, personal errands
- *Afternoons:* office time — sermon preparation, administration
- *Evenings:* personal-contact ministries

The church board was impressed. "I see," said the chairman. "It's like you're working second shift."

What do Allison's wife and young daughter think? "It took us awhile to adjust," he says, "but now we find it's very relaxing. It gives us some great opportunities we missed before. For example, I can take Heather to the public library for story time, which is offered only in the morning hours. In fact, I'm usually the only father in the room! She thinks that makes her daddy extra special.

"Then, when I go to work at midday and keep going until late at night, I don't feel like a martyr. And neither does my family."

Funding the Gift of Hospitality

Like many young couples starting in the pastorate, Don and Caroline Gerig enjoyed having people in their home. However, it often seemed that the opportunity to entertain coincided with an empty pocketbook.

More than 20 years ago, they started the habit of taking a small amount of cash from the Lord's portion of each paycheck (after their tithe had been given to the church) and putting it in a special can. They still have the same can in their kitchen today in Oak Park, Illinois, where they serve Calvary Memorial Church.

"Many times we go to that can to buy some groceries or to meet someone at a restaurant on the spur of the moment," say the Gerigs. "At other times, the very presence of money in this little can has been a prod to get together with someone or invite them into our home . . . after all, the money is there to be used! It has been a great help to us in exercising a ministry of hospitality."

Lunch in the Bag

Debi McComas, like many Americans, keeps a stockpile of emergency food — only she can't seem to leave it alone. That's because, as pastor's wife of the Seventh-day Adventist church in Astoria, Oregon, she faces something far more certain than nuclear disaster: drop-in company.

"At church, I'll start talking to a first-time visitor," she says, "and realize that this person really wants to talk about spiritual things. Or someone will show up unexpectedly and need to be entertained. The only thing to say is 'Come over to our place.' "

For those occasions, the McComases keep a bag filled with canned vegetables, instant potatoes, spaghetti and sauce, boxed skillet dinners, and large cans of fruit juice in the back of the cupboard. "It's gotten me out of many a bad situation over the last three years," says Debi. "I've used the emergency sack on an average of once every two months."

It has especially saved the day when the need arose at the end of a month, with cupbords nearly depleted. "Instead of complaining to my husband all the way home — 'What am I supposed to feed them?' — I've been able to put something on the table right away and concentrate instead on ministry to our guests."